Procreation and Parenthood

Procreation and Parenthood

The Ethics of Bearing and Rearing Children

Edited by
David Archard and David Benatar

CLARENDON PRESS · OXFORD

OXFORD
UNIVERSITY PRESS

Great Clarendon Street, Oxford OX2 6DP

Oxford University Press is a department of the University of Oxford.
It furthers the University's objective of excellence in research, scholarship,
and education by publishing worldwide in

Oxford New York

Auckland Cape Town Dar es Salaam Hong Kong Karachi
Kuala Lumpur Madrid Melbourne Mexico City Nairobi
New Delhi Shanghai Taipei Toronto

With offices in

Argentina Austria Brazil Chile Czech Republic France Greece
Guatemala Hungary Italy Japan Poland Portugal Singapore
South Korea Switzerland Thailand Turkey Ukraine Vietnam

Oxford is a registered trade mark of Oxford University Press
in the UK and in certain other countries

Published in the United States
by Oxford University Press Inc., New York

British Library Cataloguing in Publication Data

Data available

Library of Congress Cataloging in Publication Data

Data available

Typeset by SPI Publisher Services, Pondicherry, India
Printed in Great Britain
on acid-free paper by
MPG Books Group, Bodmin and King's Lynn

ISBN 978-0-19-959070-4

1 3 5 7 9 10 8 6 4 2

Preface

Procreation and parenting are momentous human activities. They involve the creation of new lives and then, when done appropriately, the protection and nurturing of those lives until, all going well, they become independent adults. The immense significance of these activities is all too often obscured by their frequency. Millions of children are brought into existence each year and there are billions of children who are being (or in need of being) reared. The moral significance of activities that are as common as these and that are readily open, at the very least, to anybody with functional genitals, is routinely underestimated.

This volume is an addition to the growing philosophical literature on these topics. We make no claims to comprehensiveness. No book of reasonable length could do that, and this volume is slimmer than many. Instead, our aim is to add new contributions on the twin topics of procreation and parenthood, thereby augmenting the existing literature with some novel papers.

To compensate for the specialized nature of the chapters in this book, our Introduction is intended to situate these contributions in the broader body of philosophical writing on the two areas covered by this collection. Those who are already intimately familiar with this philosophical terrain will find less need for the overview, but others may find our map useful.

We are grateful to our co-contributors to this volume. They have written on related topics before and we appreciate their willingness to contribute new work for this collection. Special thanks also go to Avery Kolers, a reader for Oxford University Press, who provided detailed and extremely insightful comments on multiple drafts of most of the chapters. Our contributors have indicated their own thanks to him, but we add ours.

Finally, Tim Bayne's chapter criticizes the views of one of us (D.B.). While philosophers tend to prefer having their views criticized to having their views ignored, they are also tempted to respond to criticism. In this case, the temptation has been resisted, at least in this book. This is motivated by the judgement that it would be better to respond in a volume of which one is not the (co-)editor.

D.A., D.B.

Contents

Contributors

DAVID ARCHARD has been Professor of Philosophy and Public Policy at Lancaster University since 2003. Before that he taught at the Universities of Ulster and St Andrews. He has published widely in applied moral, political, and legal philosophy, especially on the topics of children, family, and state; and sexual morality and the law. He is Honorary Chair of the Society for Applied Philosophy.

TIM BAYNE is University Lecturer in Philosophy of Mind at the University of Oxford and a Fellow of St Catherine's College. He is an editor of the *Oxford Companion to Consciousness*, and the author of *The Unity of Consciousness* (OUP, forthcoming).

DAVID BENATAR is Professor and Head of Philosophy at the University of Cape Town. He is the author of *Better Never to Have Been: The Harm of Coming into Existence* (Oxford, 2006).

ELIZABETH BRAKE is an associate professor of philosophy at the University of Calgary. She has published articles on moral and political aspects of marriage and of fatherhood, on feminism and Rawls, and on Kant and Hegel. She is currently completing a book manuscript on marriage in moral and political philosophy.

COLIN M. MACLEOD is an associate professor in philosophy and law at the University of Victoria. His research focuses on issues in contemporary moral, political, and legal theory with a special focus on the following topics: (1) distributive justice and equality; (2) children, families, and justice; and (3) democratic ethics. He is the author of *Liberalism, Justice, and Markets: A Critique of Liberal Equality* (OUP, 1998) and co-editor with David Archard of *The Moral and Political Status of Children* (OUP, 2002).

MICHAEL PARKER is Professor of Bioethics and Director of the Ethox Centre at the University of Oxford. His main research interest is in the ethical and social dimensions of collaborative global health research. Since 2001, Michael has coordinated the Genethics Club, a national ethics forum for health professionals and genetics laboratory staff in the United Kingdom to discuss the ethical issues arising in their day-to-day practice.

1

Introduction

DAVID BENATAR AND DAVID ARCHARD

Procreation is not the only way to become a parent, at least if we avoid an overly narrow understanding of 'parent' as 'procreator'. Nor does procreation always result in parenting, if we understand 'parenting' to involve rearing children rather than merely conceiving or bearing them. Nevertheless, procreation is the most common way of becoming a parent and those who rear children are usually those who brought them into existence. Even where those who bear children are not those who rear them, it is obviously the case that procreation is necessary for parenting. Nobody can rear children unless either they or others have brought them into existence.

This book is concerned with the ethics of procreation and of parenthood, and of the relationship between them. It does not aim to be exhaustive. That is to say, it does not aim to examine every moral issue or even every major moral issue pertaining to the ethics of procreation and parenthood. No volume of reasonable length could hope to do that. Instead, the component chapters constitute new contributions to some key questions in the area. In this Introduction, we provide an overview of the ethics of procreation and parenthood, which both contextualizes the contributors' chapters and also refers to some of the extant literature on the topic. We also offer a brief conspectus of the chapters. Some chapters are concerned with the ethics of creating life, and others with the ethics of providing parental care for the children who have been created. Our Introduction addresses, first, the ethics of procreation and, second, the ethics of parenthood.

Procreation

It seems unlikely that most procreation is the product of decisions to bring new people into existence. Instead, it is usually merely a consequence of sex. That so little thought is given to procreation implies nothing about the desirability of this state of affairs. Bringing new people into existence raises many important ethical questions and it would thus be preferable if people at least thought about these before deciding to procreate.

Procreation consists of conceiving, gestating, and giving birth to children. The conception component is usually effected by means of sexual intercourse between a fertile male and female. However, it can also be achieved by means of artificial insemination or *in vitro*. It usually involves the union of a sperm and ovum. However, understood more broadly, it can also include cloning. Gestation, given the current technological limits, must take place *in vivo* (except for the earliest stages of division in cases where fertilization or the equivalent is *in vitro*). In the future 'artificial wombs' might be developed. This would preclude the necessity of a woman gestating a foetus. If that ever happens then nobody will 'give birth' to the affected foetuses. One might argue that these foetuses would still be 'delivered', but delivery would take a quite different form.

Although procreation consists of the aforementioned three stages, it usually hinges on one primary *act:* the sexual act in which the new person is conceived.[1] Gestation follows and although one could decide to perform an action that terminates the pregnancy,[2] there

---

[1] In assisted reproduction the number of acts required to initiate a pregnancy increases. Thus e.g. sperm and ova may be harvested, fertilized in vitro, and then implanted in the uterus.

[2] There is an extensive and rich philosophical literature on the ethics of abortion. This volume does not add to it.

is no specific action or set of actions that constitute gestation. (There are actions that can either facilitate or impede the successful gestation of a healthy foetus.) In cases of vaginal delivery, childbirth involves some action. The woman giving birth employs her pelvic muscles to hasten birth once labour has begun. Delivery of a child is also active, particularly when there is a complication or where a caesarean section is necessary.

'Natural' versus 'Artificial' Reproduction

Some people believe that a necessary condition for procreation's being morally acceptable is that it be 'natural', where the relevant sense of 'natural' is the opposite of 'artificial'. This requirement does not preclude all assistance in reproduction. Prescribing a pharmacological treatment for erectile dysfunction, for example, may assist a couple in reproducing naturally. What the 'natural' requirement does preclude is any 'artificial' component in the process of conceiving or implanting a child.[3] Thus artificial insemination (that is, insemination by non-penile means), *in vitro* fertilization, or cloning,[4] followed by implantation, are thought, on this

---

[3] Joseph Ratzinger and Alberto Bovone, 'Instruction on Respect for Human Life and its Origin and on the Dignity of Procreation: Replies to Certain Questions of the Day'. <http://www.vatican.va/roman_curia/congregations/cfaith/documents/rc_con_cfaith_doc_19870222_respect-for-human-life_en.html> (accessed Apr. 2008):

the generation of a child must therefore be the fruit of that mutual giving...which is realized in the conjugal act wherein the spouses cooperate as servants and not as masters in the work of the Creator who is Love. In reality, the origin of a human person is the result of an act of giving. The one conceived must be the fruit of his parents' love. He cannot be desired or conceived as the product of an intervention of medical or biological techniques; that would be equivalent to reducing him to an object of scientific technology. No one may subject the coming of a child into the world to conditions of technical efficiency which are to be evaluated according to standards of control and dominion. *The moral relevance of the link between the meanings of the conjugal act and between the goods of marriage, as well as the unity of the human being and the dignity of his origin, demand that the procreation of a human person be brought about as the fruit of the conjugal act specific to the love between spouses.* (Emphasis in the original.)

[4] Other people criticize reproductive cloning because they say that it involves treating the clone as a means rather than as an end in itself. See e.g. Kahn, 2007. Among those who defend reproductive cloning are: Harris, 1997; Benatar, 1998: 165–6; Glannon, 1998; Hershenov, 2000.

view, to be morally unacceptable. Advocates of this view can be excused for not talking about artificial gestation, given that there are currently no artificial alternatives to gestation *in utero*, although their acceptance of incubation of premature and extremely premature babies is curious. It seems that the objection is only against artificiality in the earlier stages of bearing children. This would also explain why caesarean sections, which are hardly natural, are considered unobjectionable, at least where they are medically indicated rather than merely elective. Some of those opposed to artificial reproduction may make an exception in the case of incubation and non-vaginal (read non-'natural') delivery on the grounds that these interventions save foetal lives. However, granting an exception on these grounds would require those who think that zygotic and embryonic human lives have moral standing to extend the exception to artificial implantation, for implantation would be necessary to save these very young human lives.

It is hard to see how the requirement that procreation be 'natural' could be defended. How can it make a moral difference whether the sperm enters the vagina via penis or via syringe? What moral difference can it make whether fertilization occurs *in vivo* or *in vitro*? Defenders of the 'natural' requirement think that the proximate cause of conception must be a loving sexual act. However, even if one thinks that any child conceived must be conceived by a loving couple, it is unclear why they must do this via a sexual act. Others might argue that *in vitro* fertilization and some other forms of artificial reproduction carry greater risks for the people who are thereby brought into existence. Those are reasonable concerns[5] but they do not speak unequivocally against artificial reproduction and in favour of natural reproduction. Sometimes reproducing naturally carries higher risks for the resultant people. If the procreators are carriers of a serious genetic abnormality, *in vitro* fertilization, followed by pre-implantation genetic

---

[5]   Hansen *et al.*, 2002; Schieve *et al.*, 2002; Sutcliffe and Ludwig, 2007.

diagnosis and selective implantation, will be less risky even once one factors in any dangers of *in vitro* fertilization itself.

Procreation and Marriage

A restriction that is more commonly thought to apply to procreation is that it must take place within the context of marriage or, at least, a loving relationship. The claim that procreation may only take place within the context of a loving relationship is distinct from the claim that *sex* may only take place within such a context. Although the latter view implies the former in all those cases where procreation is effected by sexual means, no such implication exists where procreation is achieved without sex.

The requirement that *procreation* is permissible only within a loving relationship, where it is not mysterious, is justified with reference to the interests of the child who will result. It is said that children are disadvantaged if they are reared by a single parent. This justification for a restriction on procreation appeals to an implication for rearing. Accordingly, insofar as procreation is intentionally separated from rearing the resultant children, as it is in gamete donation and gestational surrogacy, this particular justification for the restriction on procreation cannot be invoked. To be sure, there are other objections that may be raised against these practices. Some have argued that gestational surrogacy is exploitative of the surrogate, or commodifies her body, or commodifies the baby that is then 'sold' to the commissioning parents.[6] Others, noting the value of genetic connections with one's parents and siblings,[7] have argued that gamete donation violates a child's

---

[6] Anderson, 1990. For alternative views, see Macklin, 1988: 57–64; Malm, 1989.

[7] Some of the benefit of a genetic connection with one's parents and siblings is psychological. Many adopted people want to seek out their genetic parents (and siblings). There are sometimes also medical benefits. A family history can provide people with information about their own disease risks and sometimes help in assist in predictive testing and in diagnosis.

interest in being reared by its genetic parents. Another objection to
gamete donation is that it almost always undertaken too lightly.[8]

Many of those who think that procreation is only permissible
within the context of a loving relationship have a rather narrow
view of which loving relationships qualify. They seek to exclude
same-sex couples, arguing that it is wrong for them to procreate
(with the assistance they would obviously require). Because gay
couples who procreate intend to raise the resultant children within
the context of a loving relationship, the objection to their procreation must either rest on its (already discussed) artificiality or on the
common claim that being raised by gay parents is bad for children.
Three reasons are given for the latter claim. The first is that children
need to have a parent of each sex in order to thrive. The second is
that children reared by homosexuals are more likely to be homosexual. Neither claim is supported by the available evidence.[9]
Moreover, the second claim, even if it were true, would constitute
a reason against gays rearing children only if homosexuality were
undesirable. A third reason for suggesting that being raised by gay
parents is bad for children is that homosexual unions are more likely
to break up, and children do less well when parents split.[10] We are
unaware of any evidence in support of this claim.[11] However, even
if it were true, this would not by itself entail that it is morally
impermissible for gays (and gays alone) to rear children. A mere
elevation of risk is insufficient to make the case. The risk and the
risked harm would have to be substantial. It would also have to be
the case that we were unable to make more fine-grained distinc-
tions between those gay couples who are and those who are not

---

More rarely, where one requires a matched marrow or organ donor, a connection with one's
genetic family can sometimes mean the difference between life and death.

[8] Benatar, 1999. See also Weinberg, 2008.

[9] Green, 1992: 19–23; Baetens and Brewaeys, 2001: 512–19.

[10] This argument is advanced by Almond, 2006: 109.

[11] Brenda Almond cites the New Hampshire *Commission to Study all Aspects of Same Sex
Civil Marriage and the Legal Equivalents Thereof, Whether Referred to as Civil Unions, Domestic
Partnerships, or Otherwise, SB 427*, ch. 100:2, *Laws of 2004*. However, that document, as far as
we can see, merely asserts this claim without providing evidence for it.

more likely to part. We would have to balance the elevated risks against the interests (some) homosexuals have in parenting. Finally, we would have to treat prospective homosexual parents no differently from other categories of people who are at similar risks of splitting up.

None of the essays in this book examine either the 'naturalness' or the 'loving relationships' requirements for procreation. Instead, the essays focus on much more interesting concerns about the ethics of procreation.

Future Possible People

The ethics of procreation is plagued by a special kind of problem, a problem that arises from the obvious fact that only in the case of procreative decisions do we contemplate whether or not to bring somebody into existence. Whereas other ethical choices can affect the quality of somebody's life, only procreative choices can affect whether or not somebody ever lives.

The resultant problem can be described in a variety of ways. Under one description, the problem is whether we can ever either harm or benefit anybody by bringing him into existence. Although it is tempting to offer an affirmative answer where the person brought into existence will have a life of suffering, justifying such an answer is difficult. Ordinarily we understand harm and benefit, respectively, as making somebody worse or better off than he would have otherwise have been. The problem is that he could not have been worse (or better) off if he had not been brought into existence, for the simple reason that he would not have been at all. Thus, although a life of suffering is bad, there seems to be a problem with saying that it is worse than the alternative of never existing, at least if the life, despite its suffering, is worth living.

Under another description, the problem is one of identifying the person to whom a duty to procreate or not to procreate can be owed. It is natural to think that such a duty could be owed to the person we could create, but again there is a problem. One can have duties to people who do exist. One can also have duties to those who, irrespective of what one does, will exist later. Opinion is somewhat more divided on whether one can have duties to those who did once exist but who have now ceased existing. However, even that kind of case is not as difficult as the case of procreation. This is because it seems extremely odd to say that one could have a duty to somebody who will never exist. There *is* nobody to whom such a duty could be owed. Now it might seem that this problem confronts only those cases where one decides not to procreate, for it is only in such cases that the potential person never becomes actual. However, there is also a difficulty in explaining how one could have a duty to bring into existence somebody who would never have existed if one had breached the purported duty, because then there would be no aggrieved party. Put another way, it is difficult to say that anybody could have a right to be brought into existence or not to be brought into existence, precisely because before we bring anybody into existence there is nobody who could enjoy such rights.

The courts have long been impressed by this problem[12] and have thus resisted finding in favour of wrongful life claims[12]—claims brought against parents or doctors by, or on behalf of, those who are alleged to have lives so bad that they should not have been started. Similarly, many philosophers have argued that whereas we may be able to explain impersonally why some reproductive choices are wrong, because they increase suffering in the world, we are unable to explain that wrong in what has become known as 'person-affecting' terms.[13] That is to say, although bringing somebody into existence may sometimes be wrong, it cannot be wrong, the argument goes, because of what it does to that person.

---

[12] For further details of US cases, see Bell and Loewer, 1985: 127–45, and Steinbock, 1992: 115–17.

[13] Parfit, 1984: 351–79.

Not everybody regards these problems as insurmountable. A number of philosophers have attempted to explain how one could either harm or benefit somebody by bringing him into existence.[14] They do so either by suggesting alternative conceptions of harm and benefit, or by denying that for somebody to be harmed or benefited, they must exist in the counterfactual case.

In his contribution to this volume, Tim Bayne provides a map of the current thinking about the ethics of bringing people into existence. He rejects what he calls the 'no-fault' view, whereby procreative decisions, on account of the problem we have outlined, cannot be morally judged, at least in terms of the interests of the person who is brought into existence. He then distinguishes between two views that maintain that procreative decisions can be evaluated with reference to the interests of the person who is brought into existence. According to one of these—what he calls the 'parity' view—decisions about which lives are worth starting must be made according to the same standard as decisions about which lives are worth continuing. The alternative position—which he dubs the 'dual-benchmark' view—maintains that different standards should be used to make decisions about which lives are worth starting and which lives are worth continuing. Tim Bayne argues for the parity view over the dual-benchmark view.

Reproductive Freedom

The interests of future possible people, if they count, are one important factor influencing a right to reproductive freedom. Insofar as our procreative actions wrongfully harm these people, they may appropriately be restricted, thereby limiting a right to reproductive freedom. However, the interests of future possible people are not the only factors to consider when determining the scope and strength of a right to reproductive freedom. The interests of

---

[14] See e.g. Feinberg, 1992: 3–36.

present people, as well as those future people who will exist independently of one's own reproductive choices are also relevant. The idea that people have a right to reproductive freedom is a popular one. This does not obviate the need to justify it. Some have sought to ground the right in a more general right to autonomy.[15] Others have suggested that there are distinctively important human interests that a right to reproductive freedom protects, and have thus sought to ground the right in those interests.[16]

Those who accept that there is a right to reproductive freedom can and do disagree about who has the right, what the scope of the right is, and how strong it is. In his contribution to this volume, David Benatar argues that the right, although important, must be limited in the same way that other rights are limited.

A right to reproductive freedom may be understood as a moral right or as a legal right. Those who think that one has a moral right to reproductive freedom may take that as a basis for thinking that there ought also to be a legal right. However, to deny that one has, in some instance, a moral right to reproductive freedom is compatible with thinking that one ought nonetheless to have a legal right. There may be good reasons for legally protecting a right to reproductive freedom that allows at least some instances of morally problematic procreation. For example, the moral costs of restricting the legal right may be still greater than allowing some reproductive discretion, even where that discretion may sometimes be abused. Thus, criticizing a couple's reproductive choices is compatible with their having a legal right to reproductive freedom. By contrast, if they have a moral right to make a reproductive choice, they cannot be faulted morally for making their choice in the way they do.

A right to reproductive freedom, whether it is a moral or legal right, consists of a right to reproduce and a right not to reproduce. It does not follow, especially in the case of the moral right, that each

---

[15] Dworkin, 1993.
[16] Robertson, 1994: 24–5.

of these component rights is equally extensive or equally strong.[17] Most people think, for example, that whereas we have a duty not to create suffering people we do not have a corresponding duty to create happy people. That asymmetry will differentially affect the two components of the general right to reproductive freedom. The existence of a duty sometimes not to procreate is incompatible with a (moral) right to procreate in those circumstances. If there is no duty to create happy people, then the right not to reproduce will not be restricted in a parallel way.

Disability and Enhancement

Many people assume that, at the very least, we may use our reproductive freedom to avoid bringing into existence those people who will be diseased or disabled, given the lower quality of life they can be expected to have. Most people go further, maintaining that we have a *duty* to avoid bringing diseased and disabled people into existence. On this view, any moral right to reproductive freedom does not include a right knowingly or negligently to bring into existence a seriously diseased or disabled person.

Those holding these views are often taken aback by the claim, advanced by disability rights advocates, that it is morally impermissible to avoid bringing disabled people into existence (where the disability is not so bad as to make death preferable).[18] The objection is not merely against some controversial means, such as abortion, of avoiding disabled people. Indeed, many disability rights advocates are in other circumstances pro-choice. They believe that a woman

---

[17] Some even deny that there is a right *to* reproduce. See e.g. Floyd and Pomerantz, 1981: 131–8. Carol Kates (2004) thinks that either reproductive liberty is not 'a fundamental human right' or at least 'not an indefeasible right'.

[18] Erik Parens and Adrienne Asch, 'The Disability Rights Critique of Prenatal Testing: Reflections and Recommendations', in Parens and Asch, 2000: 3–43; Marsha Saxton, 'Why Members of the Disability Community Oppose Prenatal Diagnosis and Selective Abortion', ibid. 147–64; Adrienne Asch, 'Why I Haven't Changed My Mind about Prenatal Diagnosis: Reflections and Refinements', ibid. 234–58.

may decide that she does not wish to be pregnant or to have a baby and thus may abort. Their objection, then, is not to abortion *per se*, but rather only to the abortion of foetuses who will grow into disabled or diseased people. In other words, they have no objection to abortion where a woman does not want any baby, but they object to abortion where a woman does not want a particular baby because it will be disabled. Whereas many people are more concerned about the abortion of healthy foetuses, the disability rights advocates are more concerned about the abortion of disabled foetuses. They are also concerned about other means for avoiding the existence of disabled people.

It is tempting to dismiss this objection as mad, but there is more to it than first meets the eye. One argument advanced by disability rights advocates is based on the 'social construction of disability'. Although the disabled have impairments—they are unable to do things (such as see, hear, or walk) that others can do—these in-abilities only become disabilities because of the way society is constructed. By analogy the inability of humans to fly (unaided) is not a disability, because society is not constructed in a way that disadvantages those with an inability to fly. (For example, buildings have stairs and elevators, rather than landing pads or portholes to access higher floors.) There are obvious reasons why the social construction disadvantages relatively uncommon inabilities but not common or universal ones. Nevertheless, it remains true that if society were constructed differently, those who are currently disabled by their inabilities would not be. Once the discriminatory nature of society is understood, disability rights advocates are able to draw an analogy with sexist or racist societies, which disable women or people of some 'races'. We might reasonably be concerned about sex selection in sexist societies, even though it is true that those girls whose existence is thereby prevented will have lived lives that are worse than those of their brothers.[19] The appro-priate response, it is commonly thought, is not to avoid the birth of

---

[19]   For more on sex selection, see Warren, 1985; and Holmes, 1995.

girls, but rather to alter the society in such a way that being female is no longer a disadvantage. Indeed, avoiding the birth of girls is thought to contribute to the society's sexism.

Another disability rights argument against interventions aimed at preventing the birth of disabled people maintains that these interventions arise from underestimates of the quality of disabled lives. People living with these disabilities, the argument goes, usually think that their lives are worth living. It is thus presumptuous of others to think that they know better what the quality of these lives is. A related argument objects that interventions to prevent disabled lives implicitly express the insulting view that those existing people with the same disabilities should have been prevented—that there should not be people like that around.

These disability rights arguments are not without their critics.[20] For example, it is, at the very least, controversial whether being female really is a good analogy for being blind or mentally retarded. And it may be the case that those living with disabilities (like everybody else) are overestimating, rather than others underestimating, the quality of their lives.[21] In any event, if, contrary to what Tim Bayne suggests, we evaluate future lives according to a higher standard than present lives, one could seek to prevent disabled lives without thinking that this implies anything about the lives of existing disabled people.

Even more controversial than the claim that it is wrong to aim at the avoidance of disabled people are attempts to aim at *having* a child with a disability. A few deaf people have sought interventions that will either guarantee or maximize the chance of having a deaf child.[22] Their argument, which is much more compelling in the case of deafness than it would be in the case of other disabilities, is that they want their child to be fully and unambiguously part of

---

[20] Buchanan *et al.*, 2000: 258–303; James Lindemann Nelson, 'The Meaning of the Act: Reflections on the Expressive Force of Reproductive Decision Making and Policies', in Parens and Asch, 2000: 196–213.

[21] Benatar, 2006: 118–22.

[22] Levy, 2002; McLellan, 2002.

their linguistic community, a community in which they, like the speakers of many other languages, take pride. Although hearing children could also sign, they would be much more likely to drift into the vernacular and to become effectively second-language users of Sign (even if it were also their home-language). The parents' interest in having their children be full members of their linguistic community is an important one. However, it must also be weighed against the children's interests in participating in the broader society in which they find themselves. For example, Spaniards in England may well have an interest in their children speaking Spanish, but for them to prevent their children from being able to speak English is to close off important options for those children.

Michael Parker, in his contribution to this book, briefly mentions some of these disability issues. However, his focus is on responding to an argument that comes from the other end of the spectrum—an argument for 'procreative beneficence'.[23] According to this principle, we have a duty not merely to avoid disability but to produce the very best children we can.[24] It is a consequence of this view that if we can employ enhancement techniques, whether genetic or environmental, to produce better children than we otherwise would, we ought to do so. This view stands in opposition not only to the disability rights views already outlined, but also to more common views that whereas therapies are morally acceptable or even required, enhancements are impermissible. On this view, there is something odious about seeking to produce 'designer babies'.[25]

Some arguments against enhancement are better than others. For example, where the enhancement, such as increased height, is only

---

[23] Julian Savulescu (2001) is one defender of procreative beneficence.

[24] As Allen Buchanan *et al.* note, the very strong view that we have a *duty* to produce the best children possible can be distinguished from a weaker view that it is morally *desirable* or *good* (rather than strictly required) to produce the best children, and from an even weaker claim that we are *permitted* to take steps to produce the best children we can. See Buchanan *et al.*, 2000: 161–3.

[25] One recent exponent of this view is Sandel, 2007.

an advantage relative to others, the following problem arises. If everybody seeks and gains the enhancement, nobody will actually be better off. Everybody will be taller, for example, but the relative advantage over others will be lost.[26] And if only some have access to and attain the enhancement, then given that they are most likely already to be among the more privileged, there may be something unjust about allowing them this further advantage over others.[27]

The justice concern also confronts enhancements that are intrinsic benefits rather than merely relative advantages, although it seems more mean-spirited to deny an intrinsic benefit merely because others cannot enjoy it too. Moreover, because the advantage of intrinsic benefits is not lost where others enjoy them too, the 'arms-race' argument cannot be advanced against such enhancements.

Some opponents of genetic enhancements are not opposed to non-genetic enhancements. They must show why it is acceptable to improve children via nutrition, rearing, education, but not via genetic and other prenatal interventions that may have similar effects. Those opponents of genetic enhancements who also oppose some non-genetic enhancements avoid this problem. Whether their view is tenable depends on whether they can explain why some enhancements, whether genetic or otherwise, are permissible while others are not. Michael Parker's objection to procreative beneficence is different. He raises some interesting objections and suggests that we should set our sights a little lower, and aim only at producing children that have 'a reasonable chance of a good life'.

Parenthood

Once children are brought into existence they need, in virtue of their vulnerable and dependent natures, to be reared. Who then should be a child's parent? This second half of the 'Introduction'

---

[26] Buchanan *et al.*, 2000: 185.
[27] Ibid. 187–91. See also Glannon, 2001: 97–9.

provides a critical overview of the ethics of parenthood. Here we supply a map of the different issues that any full ethical account of parenthood would need to address, and we locate the contributions that follow within that map. To anticipate: the contributions of David Archard and Elizabeth Brake address the particular question of how one gets to be a parent, whereas that of Colin Macleod is concerned with how the special duties of parents fit with the broader demands of social justice.

A preliminary note on terminology is in order. The terms 'duties', 'obligations', and 'responsibilities' can be employed more or less interchangeably. Some of our contributors do so, as do others who write in this area. However we recognize that the term 'responsibilities' might seem not to have the same implications that the other terms do. For example, by comparison with 'duties' or 'obligations', 'responsibilities' can be specified in terms that accord more discretion to those who must discharge them and that show less concern for the achievement of specific outcomes. It may also be, as David Archard argues in his chapter, that we should distinguish between the obligation or duty that falls on someone to ensure that a child is cared for and the responsibilities of actually caring for the child. The former imposes a clear and stringent requirement that the child is provided with a minimally decent upbringing. The person who does care for the child will nevertheless have considerable discretion in the ways that the child is actually brought up, and will not be bound to achieve any particular, well-defined upshot. We have opted for the use of parental 'duties' throughout this Introduction and left to one side the important philosophical questions that are raised by the use of the different terms.

A child—for instance, a neglected orphan—might not have parents. We can also envisage collective or social arrangements for the rearing of every child. A useful distinction is between a 'family state' and a 'state of families'.[28] The first kind of state assumes

[28] Gutmann, 1987: ch. 1.

complete responsibility for the shaping of its future members whereas the second devolves responsibility for the care and rearing of children to families. In the history of philosophy Plato and Locke are, respectively, the best-known defenders of each state.[29]

In *The Republic* Plato defends the collective rearing of children, albeit only for the children of the Republic's ruling class, 'The Guardians'. Plato defends such an arrangement principally as a means of ensuring that the loyalties of the Guardians to the state are not diverted or diluted in consequence of any attachments to their children. His suggested arrangements—involving both the eugenic selection of suitable procreative partners and the rearing of children in official nurseries—also ensure the reproduction of the best possible future Guardians.

By contrast John Locke defends a view of parents as those whose role is a fiduciary one, having temporary tutelage of their offspring, and being charged with the responsibility of bringing the child (born *to* the state of equality enjoyed by their parents but not yet *in* that state) to the full possession of reason and independence. Locke denies that his own famous theory of property applies to the relationship between parents and children; indeed he thinks of parents not so much as having rights over the young but as enjoined to care for them.[30]

Although no philosophers of note have subsequently endorsed Plato's collectivism, the basic aim of abolishing the family in the service of loyalty to the state and public ends has found support from both fascist and communist regimes.[31] That aim is fairly characterized as totalitarian and Plato, in consequence, is frequently caricatured as a proto-totalitarian thinker.[32] It is also common to

---

[29] Plato *The Republic* 5. 457–64, 8. 543a; *Timaeus* 18c; John Locke, *Two Treatises of Government*, I, chs. II, VI, and IX: §89; and II, ch. VI.

[30] For further discussion of Locke's views, see Archard, 1998.

[31] Ferdinand Mount, a conservative traditionalist, thus characterizes the family as a subversive institution which has been attacked by authoritarian regimes of both right and left. See Mount, 1982: ch. 2, 'The State and the Family'.

[32] Popper, 2002.

think, as a corollary, that the defence of the family as an institution standing between the individual and the state is an essential commitment of liberalism.

There was radical criticism of the family in the 1960s but as part of a more general countercultural dissatisfaction with long-established conventional social forms.[33] It was less the family as such than a particular form of it which was under attack: the monogamous, married heterosexual couple bringing up their own biological offspring to inherit property and traditional social values. Yet at a minimum the family is merely a cohabiting group of some adults and some children, the former being accorded a role of parental guardianship over the latter during their minority, and as a consequence enjoying a degree of protected privacy for their shared lives. Such a definition leaves open questions of the number of adults, their married status, sexual preferences, and the provenance of their relation to the children. It thus exempts the family, and the institution of parenthood, from criticisms properly directed at particular familial forms.

Who Gets to be a Parent of Which Child?

A general negative case in favour of the family may acknowledge its failings but note the awfulness, and perhaps unfeasibility, of alternatives such as 'Platonic' collectivism. Such a case for the family may thus be akin to Churchill's famous 'defence' of democracy as 'the worst form of government, except for all those other forms that

---

[33] Such criticism was very varied. It included the anthropologist Edmund Leach's infamous description of the family 'with its narrow privacy and tawdry secrets' as 'the source of all our discontents', in his Reith Lectures (*The Listener*, 20 Nov. 1967), the poet Philip Larkin's claim in verse that parents 'fuck you up' ('This be the Verse', (1971) in Larkin, 2003), the claim of anti-psychiatrists such as R. D. Laing that that mental illness could be attributed to dysfunctional families (Laing and Esterson, 1970), in addition to assorted socialist and feminist critiques (Barrett and McIntosh, 1991).

have been tried from time to time'.[34] A positive case, by contrast, may appeal to the interests and values the family serves.

A general defence of the family, whether a negative or positive one, is nevertheless limited in scope. It may answer the question whether children should have parents—particular adults entrusted with their exclusive care—or whether there should be a system of collectivized rearing. If that question is answered in favour of the family, there are two further questions which need answering: (a) which adults get to be parents? And (b) which children are brought up by which parents?

Answers to these two questions must accommodate the interests of three different parties: children, as dependent and vulnerable humans, require an assurance of adequate care and protection; adults have very strong interests in being able to bring up children; and society as a whole has an interest in its own future being assured. We need not presume that all adults are possible prospective parents. Indeed the view that parenting can be a dangerous activity—for the children at least—and thus in need of licensing has been defended by some, and entertained as a possibility by policy-makers.[35] Note that licensing procedures can serve to answer either (a) or (b) of the questions identified above. In response to the question of which adults get to be parents the licensing procedure requires a demonstration of a threshold level of parental competence. In response to the second question of which children are brought up by which parents the procedure works to select the most appropriate adult guardians for each and every child.

What we might term *a conception of parenthood* specifies what rights are held and what duties are owed in respect of some particular child by which adults. Further, it offers an account of the relevant facts that ground those rights and duties. A conception of parenthood provides an answer to question (b) above. The facts

---

[34] Speech in the House of Commons (11 Nov. 1947).
[35] LaFollette, 1980. Further treatments of the idea can be found in Westman, 1994; Irvine, 2003; Tittle, 2004.

which are specified by a particular conception of parenthood may identify a relationship between the adult and the child. For instance, the causal account of parenthood holds that someone has the rights and duties of a parent in respect of the child that he or she causes to exist. By contrast an intentional account of parenthood holds that someone becomes a parent of a particular child only as the result of voluntary undertakings in respect of that child. Yet the facts need not identify any particular relationship between the adult and child. Imagine a parental lottery which randomly distributes children, after they are born, to all those who have indicated a wish and demonstrated an ability to be a parent.[36]

A conception of parenthood may be justified in two quite different ways. A direct justification points to facts which are true of some individual and which suffice to establish that the individual has a claim over a child or is responsible for a child. By contrast, an indirect justification points to the claims that individuals can make within and by reference to the ends of the institution of parenthood which is itself given a prior justification. In effect the direction of the justification is different in each. On a direct account individuals have rights over or duties in respect of children, and the institution of parenthood must be constituted to give effect to these normative claims. By contrast an indirect account offers a justification of the institution of parenthood by pointing to the valued ends it serves— such as, for instance, the protection of and care for otherwise vulnerable children. A justification of this kind leaves open the further and logically subsequent questions of who gets to be a parent, and who gets to parent which particular children.

The question of who gets to parent whom can then be answered on an indirect account in various ways. For example, we might simply use a lottery to allocate children after birth to particular parents. Or we could use biological parenthood as the relevant basis for allocation. This scheme in turn might be justified either because

---

[36] For an intriguing and provocative defence of the lottery as a fair means of distributing social goods and burdens, see Goodwin, 2005.

facts of origin are salient ones, or because it is felt that biological parents tend best to promote the ends of the institution of parenthood.

In sum a direct account of parenthood justifies the institution of parenthood in terms of prior or pre-institutional claims made by or of individuals; whereas an indirect account of parenthood first justifies the institution of parenthood and then distributes parental roles within that institution, tending to do so in terms that are consonant with the valued ends of the institution as a whole.[37] Most conceptions of parenthood justify it directly and on the grounds of facts that identify relevant relationships between the adults and the children.

How does a conception of parenthood work? It identifies those persons who have rights over and duties in respect of some child in virtue of certain facts. For instance, a particular conception of parenthood may hold that person A has a certain set of rights over child B and owes duties to child B, and does so because A is B's biological father. Any conception of parenthood thus comprises both normative claims and the identification of certain relevant facts. The distinction in respect of parenthood between normative claims and factual assertions is often expressed by claiming that there are different senses of 'parent'. Thus one might define a causal parent as that person who, as a matter of fact, caused the child to come into existence. A moral parent is that person who has a warranted claim to care for the child or from whom the child has a warranted claim for her care. A social parent is that person who, by convention, custom, or social rule, is given the role of looking after the child. A legal parent is that person whom the law—by statutory provision or a court judgement—determines to have the legally protected rights or owe the legally enforceable duties of a parent.

---

[37] For a parallel, and illuminating, distinction between a pre-institutional and institutional view of desert, see Scheffler, 2001: 16–18.

It goes without saying that one and the same person can be a parent in all these distinct senses. However most of the interesting disputes precisely concern cases in which distinct persons lay claim to be parents in these different senses. Indeed if we combine the various senses of parenthood—causal, moral, social, and legal—with the range of possible relevant facts, there will be a multiplicity of competing conceptions of parenthood.

The Rights and Duties of Parenthood

Talk thus far of parental rights and duties has proceeded on the assumption that they go together and are of roughly equal normative force. This assumption is open to challenge and it helps in this regard to consider three important theses: the 'parental package' thesis; the 'no parental rights' thesis; and the 'priority' thesis.

The 'parental package' thesis holds that a set of parental duties and a set of parental rights are both distributed together as a total package to one and the same person and for the same reason. The thesis supplies an important premise in arguments either criticizing or defending particular conceptions of parenthood. A consideration which counts in favour of or against an account of the source of parental rights (or duties) only counts against a parallel account of parental duties (or rights) if parental duties and rights go together. If they do not then reasons for or against the one are not decisive in the other case. In his contribution to this volume, David Archard identifies and criticizes different versions of the parental package view.[38]

The 'no parental rights' thesis denies that parents have any rights over their children although it allows that they do have some discretion in how they discharge the duties they have to those children.[39] If parental rights, understood as claim- and not liberty-

---

[38] Austin, 2007: ch. 3, also criticises the idea that parental rights and duties go together.
[39] Montague, 2000.

rights, are oriented towards their putative possessors, the adults, then their possession is incompatible with the discharge of their primary duties, as parents, which are oriented towards their children. The fundamental moral feature of the parent–child relationship is that parents care for, protect, and promote the well-being of their children. But if they had rights over their children then, the argument runs, they would have discretion as to *whether* or not, and not simply *how*, they should discharge this fundamental obligation.

There are, as we shall see, different views of the content of a parent's duties in respect of a child. But, whatever it might be, a parent could still, consistent with discharging those duties, make many important decisions in respect of her child—regarding the child's health care, education, religious upbringing, leisure activities, culture, reading material, holidays, and name. Moreover, if some adult does have these parental rights then they are, importantly, exclusionary. Jane's right to choose what her daughter, Sarah, does on a weekend is a right that excludes other adults from making these choices. Finally, the making of those choices serves important interests an adult has in acting as a parent.

The 'no parental rights' thesis is distinct from the 'priority' thesis, which does not deny that there are parental rights but which sees them as subordinate to parental duties.[40] The subordination of parental rights to parental duties consists in at least the following: it is in virtue of the fact that parents are bound to do certain things for their children that they have rights over them. As Locke would argue it is *because* adults must ensure that children grow into rational persons that they are allowed to determine what children can and cannot do. Further, parents make those choices for children within constraints that are constituted by those duties.

Whether parents should do more than discharge their basic duties is a controversial matter. If they should do more it is also debatable how much more they should do. Colin Macleod's chapter starts from the idea that parents do have prerogatives to advance

[40] Blustein, 1982: 104–14.

the interests of their own children, and considers the extent to which the existence of such prerogatives conflicts with the demands of justice. His view is that if the exercise of parental duties involves the use of resources whose distribution is morally tainted—because, for instance, past injustices largely explain its form—then such an exercise is morally problematic.

The new technologies of reproduction have increased the number of possible biological parents. Are there reasons to limit the numbers of those who can play the parental role? Certainly social custom and convention—at least in Western societies—has favoured a familiar two-parent family; and the law has tended to follow in society's wake. However this preference may derive historically from the importance to the standard family of marriage. In Western societies at least this has taken a non-polygamous form and thus comprised a legally enforced two-person contract. Moreover social and legal conventions have also acknowledged the claims of the members of the so-called extended family—grandparents, older siblings, uncles, and aunts—when it comes to the resolution of conflicts over parenthood. For reasons of practicality and the public good it may also make perfect sense to limit the number of individuals who can have legally recognized and enforced parental rights and duties. But if we are talking about moral rights and duties must the number be limited? Answering this question should take note of three things: the source of the rights and duties; their scope; and the nature of the interests involved. A conception of parenthood specifies the facts in virtue of which some persons have parental rights and duties. Those facts can hold only of a determinate number of persons. If, for instance, parental duties are owed to a child whom one causes to exist and in virtue of that causal role, then parental duty-holders are limited to those who played that causal role.

The number of persons who exercise a parental right or discharge a parental duty will also depend on the scope or content of the right and duty. Consider what, for instance, is owed to a child. If it is no more than the provision of a basic level of care then it is feasible that this duty can be discharged by one or two adults. If the duty is more demanding then it becomes less likely that one or two adults unaided could discharge it. Indeed an important question is how our duties to children should be distributed between their parents and the state. Finally, in specifying the number of parents it helps to identify the interests served by the rights and duties. The parental right protects the fundamental interest that an adult has in bringing up a child. The quotidian care and protection of a child, the sharing of an intimate life with a young developing human being, can only be enjoyed by a small number of adults. Indeed, at the limit, it destroys the point of being a parent (and having the parental role protected) to have to be one parent amongst many. Colin Macleod's chapter shares with important work by Adam Swift and Harry Brighouse the idea that family life realizes important values that have essentially to do with the nature of the intimate caring relationship between parents and child.[41]

Conceptions of Parenthood

What do the rights and duties of parenthood amount to? How extensive are they? Parental duties have been defined in more or less demanding ways: as a requirement to raise children so that they experience significant well-being over the course of their subsequent lives;[42] so that they have a reasonable expectation of minimally decent lives as children;[43] to promote the child's autonomy;[44] or, following Joel Feinberg's influential claim, to guarantee the child a right to an open future.[45]

[41] Brighouse and Swift, 2006: 80–108.
[42] Austin, 2007: ch. 5.
[43] O'Neill, 1979: 25–38.
[44] Bigelow et al., 1988: 3–16.
[45] See Feinberg, 1980.

As for parental rights no one now defends the absolutist presumptions of *patria potestas*, the right of a father, enshrined in Roman law, to do with his child whatever he so chose up to and including a permission to take the child's life.[46] Most contemporary specifications of parental rights understand them in fiduciary terms as the exercise of a trust or stewardship, and thus as constrained by a requirement to ensure that the child develops into an adult of the kind favoured in the preferred moral theory.

Conceptions of parenthood differ interestingly in their account of the facts in virtue of which adults have parental rights or duties. We shall not appraise these conceptions beyond briefly outlining their distinctive claims and principal challenges.[47] At the outset, we set out a number of general considerations that any conception ought to acknowledge.

First, the 'parity principle' holds that any fact by virtue of which a woman laid claim to be a parent could also be a fact in virtue of which a man with equal merit could claim to be a parent, and vice versa.[48] This principle is in fact ambiguous depending on whether or not it is physically possible that the fact could hold of both sexes. This can be illustrated by considering the gestationalist claim that it is the fact of gestating a child that serves as the ground of parenthood. Now of course if a man could gestate, and did so, then a gestationalist would have to allow, consistent with the parity principle, that any man who did so would have a valid claim to parenthood of the resultant child. But since men cannot gestate the fact which grounds parenthood cannot hold of any man. So in one sense gestationalism trivially satisfies the parity principle (if, *per impossible*, men gestated they would be parents); on another it does not (men cannot in fact gestate and thus be parents). A defender of gestationalism can claim not to violate the parity principle (in its

---

[46] MacKenzie, 1862: ch. 9; Nicholas, 1962: 65–8; Lacey, 1986: 120–44; Boswell, 1988: 58–75.

[47] There are good critical reviews of the various conceptions in: Kolers and Bayne, 2001; Bayne and Kolers, 2003 and 2006; Austin, 2007: chs. 2 and 3.

[48] Kolers and Bayne, 2001: section IV.

first guise); whereas a critic of gestationalism can take its violation of the parity principle (in its second guise) to be a decisive reason to reject that conception of parenthood.

Second, no conception should require or imply the truth of the proprietarian thesis that parents can own their children. Parental proprietarianism has had its philosophical supporters in Aristotle and Thomas Hobbes.[49] It also served to embarrass John Locke's own theory of property,[50] and has continued to exercise a wide, if not always obvious, influence.[51]

Third, as Tim Bayne and Avery Kolers have made clear, any putative ground of parenthood can be defended as a necessary condition, a necessary and sufficient, or merely a sufficient condition of parenthood.[52]

Fourth, any conception of parenthood should make it clear whether the parental package view is endorsed; consequently, whether what are offered as reasons for the conception apply to both rights and duties, or only to one of them.

Fifth, any conception of parenthood can allow for a disjunction of factual grounds (for instance, X is a parent if she is either the genetic or gestational mother) or insist upon only one kind of fact as a ground. In short parental conceptions can be either pluralist or monist.[53]

Sixth, any conception of parenthood must be able to acknowledge the new, and as yet undeveloped, possibilities of reproductive technology. A pressing problem is that of reproductive cloning. Independently of the ethics of such cloning[54] is the question of

---

[49] Aristotle, *Nicomachean Ethics* 5. 1134b; Thomas Hobbes, *Leviathan*, ch. 20, 'Of Dominion Paternall and Despotical'.

[50] Robert Nozick (1974: 174–81) provides a classic critique of Locke's difficulties in defending a non-proprietarian account of parenthood.

[51] Contemporary defences of parental proprietarianism include Narveson, 1988 and 2002: Hall, 1999. Page, 1984, defends something close to a proprietarian thesis. For critical reviews of parental proprietarianism, see Archard, 2004: 141–5, and Austin, 2007: ch. 2.

[52] Kolers and Bayne, 2001: 274; Bayne and Kolers, 2003: 222.

[53] Bayne and Kolers, 2003: 221–42.

[54] See n. 4 above.

whether any defensible conception of parenthood can either show why the person who clones herself is her clone's parent (and that this implication is not troublesome); or show that she is not her own parent (and clarify whether it is troubling that a clone might lack a parent).

Seventh, any conception of parenthood must allow for and explain—or disallow and justify the exclusion of—the waiving and transfer of normative claims. On the preferred conception, for instance, is it possible for whosoever has the rights or duties of a parent to transfer them to another? In his contribution David Archard starts from the causal theory's claim that whoever is causally responsible for the creation of a child is thereby under an obligation to ensure that the child is adequately cared for. The truth of the causal theory, which he finds plausible, is consistent with its being the case that willing others who did not cause the child to exist may take on the responsibilities of acting as parents. That in turn suggests that a conscientious and enlightened system of child abandonment may also be morally permissible.

The principal conceptions of parenthood, which have been defended in the literature, are the gestational, genetic, causal, and intentional. The claims of these theories are, in summary, as follows. The gestational account holds that a parent is such by virtue of her gestational role.[55] Such an account must meet the challenge of the parity principle and demonstrate the special significance of the gestational role in relation to other causal contributions to procreation.

A causal conception of parenthood grounds it in the causing of a child to exist. It has principally been defended as an account of parental duties.[56] The causal conception needs to meet a number of challenges. It must identify, in a non-arbitrary manner, those whose causal role in the creation of a child is such that they acquire duties

---

[55] Rothman, 1989; S. Feldman, 1992.
[56] See Nelson, 1991: 49–61; Blustein, 1997: 79–86; Mills, 2001: 183–98. For scepticism about strict parental liability, see Brake, 2005: 55–73.

to care for the child. It must answer the question of whether those who may be thought of as faultlessly causing a child to exist (those, for instance, who take all reasonable opportunities to avoid conception) nevertheless acquire parental duties. A particular problem for the causal conception is that of gamete donation. Does a gamete donor incur duties towards the future child simply in virtue of playing a causal role in that child's existence? Or is the donor permitted, in circumstances where he or she can be reasonably assured that the child's welfare is guaranteed, to relinquish both duties and rights in respect of the child?[57]

A final problem for the causal conception is the requirement that its defenders show whether there are any problematic gender asymmetries in the acquisition of parental duties. These may be thought to arise inasmuch as men and women play different causal roles in the creation of children. They also arise if women are granted, but men are not, a right to determine whether or not a pregnancy is terminated.

A genetic conception holds that those who contribute genetic material to the child thereby acquire the rights and duties of parents. Any defence of such a conception must show how it does not require or entail the proprietarian claim ('These are my genes, and hence a child which has them is mine'). It may also require defence of a contentious view of a person's identity as essentially genetic. Finally it will need to show why the contribution of genetic material is especially significant by comparison with, most obviously, what may be the non-genetic contribution of a gestational mother.

By contrast, an intentional account of parenthood grounds it in the intentions of those who seek to bring a child into existence or who demonstrate a commitment to care for the child.[58] Such an account may serve successfully to identify those who will act in the

---

[57] Amongst those who worry whether gamete donation generates parental or other duties see: Page, 1985; Callahan, 1992; Benatar, 1999; Bayne, 2003.

[58] Stumpf, 1986; Shultz, 1990; Hill, 1991.

best interests of a future or existing child. Yet it needs to show that it can account successfully for both parental rights and parental duties. Moreover, the account needs to be clear whether the converse of an intention to parent, a renunciation of such an intention or declaration of an intention not to parent, suffices to waive the parental rights or acquit one of the parental duties.

Elizabeth Brake, in her chapter, defends a version of the intentional account in respect of parental duties. She thinks that the duties of parenting a child arise, and can only arise, from voluntary acceptance of the parental role. This role is socially constituted. Elizabeth Brake finds difficulties with the causal account to which David Archard is sympathetic. In particular she thinks that it cannot explain the particular duties of moral parenthood in terms of an obligation to compensate for the creation of a helpless child. There is, she thinks, an explanatory gap between paying the costs of procreation and the socially constituted duties of a moral parent.

The ethics of procreation and of parenthood are, as this Introduction has demonstrated, complex and rich. They allow for a wide variety of distinct and contrasted viewpoints. To repeat our earlier cautionary note: the following chapters do not address, nor do they aspire to address, all of the issues that have been identified in our Introduction. However they do make original contributions to our understanding of some of the most central ones.

2

In Defence of Genethical Parity

TIM BAYNE

I

Job, so the story goes, cursed the day of his birth and the night of his conception. Whereas Job's resentment at having been brought into existence was directed at God, in contemporary life such attitudes are directed at one's parents or the medical establishment and are often played out in court. In what is known as a wrongful life case, an individual with a serious genetic disorder argues that her life is not worth living, and that she was wrongly brought into existence. Understandably, the courts have not welcomed such cases. As one court complained, 'whether it is better never to have been born at all than to have been born with even gross deficiencies is a mystery more properly to be left to the philosophers and the theologians'.[1]

I cannot speak for the theologians, but philosophers certainly have not known what to do with these questions. Following David Heyd, I will call questions that concern the nature and basis of ethical attitudes that are directed towards our coming into existence 'genethical questions'.[2] Genethical questions take a number of forms. Some focus on the *event* of a person's coming into existence; others focus on the *act* of bringing a person into existence. Some

---

[1] New York Court of Appeals *Becker* v. *Schwartz* 413 NYS 2d, 895, 900 (1978).
[2] See Heyd, 1992.

genethical questions are asked by individuals about the lives of other individuals; some are asked by individuals about their own lives. Some genethical questions take a prospective form and focus on lives that have not yet been created; others take a retrospective form and concern lives that have already begun (and indeed may already have ended). My concern here is not with the differences between various genethical questions, but with the task of developing a framework that might inform genethical theorizing whatever its orientation.

We can divide genethical models into three broad groups: *no-faults* models, *parity* models, and *dual-benchmark* models. No-faults genethicists claim that coming into existence is not properly subject to moral evaluation, at least so far as the interests of the person that is brought into existence are concerned. No-faults genethicists do not deny that it can be wrong to bring someone into existence to the extent that procreation can have adverse effects on the interests of third parties, but they hold that procreation cannot be wrong on account of the well-being of the person who is brought into existence. A no-faults genethicist denies that it can be reasonable to have any evaluative attitude—either regret or satisfaction—towards having come into existence. Parity theorists and dual-benchmark theorists share the view that it can be wrong to bring someone into existence on account of their well-being, and that it can be reasonable to regret having been created. The two positions are distinguished by where they put the genethical benchmark. To a first approximation, parity theorists insist that the level of well-being that determines whether or not a life is worth starting is identical to that which determines whether or not it is worth continuing. Dual-benchmark theorists reject parity. They hold that our genethical judgements need not—and in fact *should not*—be brought into line with our judgements about the kinds of lives that are worth sustaining. The dual-benchmark theorist posits one benchmark for starting lives and another for continuing them.

How might we decide between competing approaches to gen-ethics? I take there to be three main sources of constraint. First, any acceptable account of genethics must have some intuitive plausibility. It is a pro tanto advantage of a genethical theory that its implications are intuitively plausible, and a pro tanto disadvantage of a theory if its implications offend genethical commonsense. Secondly, an acceptable genethical account ought to comport with our intuitions in neighbouring ethical domains. Genethical judgements cannot 'float free', but must be consistent with more general ethical and metaphysical considerations. Again, it is a pro tanto advantage for a genethical theory that it is consistent with such claims, and a pro tanto disadvantage that it is inconsistent with such claims. And, thirdly, a genethical model ought to be internally consistent. As far as possible, the answers that an account of genethics gives to one type of genethical question ought to 'hang together' with the answers that it gives to another type of genethical question. With these three constraints in mind, let us consider the relative merits of the three accounts outlined above.

II

I begin with no-faults genethicism. One of the leading proponents of the no-faults position is David Heyd. In *Genethics* Heyd argues that coming into existence can be neither a harm nor a benefit. 'It is equally meaningless to resent our parents for having been born unhappy as it is to be grateful for having been born happy.'[3] Heyd thinks there is something logically problematic with the idea that one could harm or benefit someone by bringing them into existence. How could it be possible to be better off in a world in which one does not exist than one is in a world in which one does exist?[4] Indeed, how could one have any level of well-being—any level of 'offness'—in worlds from which one is absent? There might be an impersonal sense of goodness in which worlds

---

[3] Ibid. 109.
[4] Ibid. 122.

containing Job might be better than worlds that lack him, but, Heyd suggests, it makes no sense to say that such worlds are better *for Job*. For a world to be good or bad for one, one must exist within it. Heyd concludes: 'to be cannot in itself be either good or bad, a subject of duty or prohibition, a right or wrong'.[5]

No-faults genethics flies in the face of certain robust intuitions. Whether or not we think Job was justified in cursing the day of his birth, his attitude certainly seems to have been *coherent*. It seems to be possible for someone to rationally regret—or, indeed, celebrate—having come into existence. No-faults genethics also appears to be counter-intuitive when it comes to genethical actions. Consider someone who intentionally creates a child knowing that she has an extremely high chance of having a short life that consists of little more than unremitting pain. Ordinary intuition suggests that such a person has done something wrong, and that the wrongness of the act has something to do with the quality of the child's life. In short, common-sense morality strongly suggests that bringing people into existence can indeed be bad, the subject of prohibition, and a wrong.

These appeals to intuition are far from decisive, for it is arguable that any account of genethics will flout some genethical intuitions. But these worries can be buttressed by noting that the no-faults theorist appears to be committed to an Epicurean view of death. Epicureans hold that it is irrational to attach any moral or prudential value to one's own death on the grounds that one can be neither harmed nor benefited by death. Because death brings non-existence, the states of being dead and alive are incommensurable with respect to levels of welfare. The dead are neither better nor worse off than the living—they lack any degree of 'offness'. This suggests that Heyd's account of coming into existence goes hand-in-glove with an Epicurean account of going out of existence. Putting it another way, if the transition from existence to non-existence can be subject

---

[5] See Heyd, 1992: 124.

to moral evaluation why can't the transition from non-existence to existence also be subject to moral evaluation?

Heyd rejects the Epicurean view of death, and argues that there are two important differences between coming into existence and going out of existence. The first difference is that death has a subject, 'an identifiable individual whose life is cut short contrary to his or her interests',[6] whereas there is no identifiable individual who is brought from non-existence into existence: identity is always subsequent to existence. We can say of someone who died that she was deprived of her future, but we cannot say of a possible person who was not brought into existence that she was deprived of existence, for only in the former case do we have an actual subject of harm.

It is of course true that death necessarily involves a subject who is harmed. And it is also true that possible people who are not brought into existence are not deprived of existence. No one is (directly) harmed by the decision not to instantiate a good life; and, correlatively, no one is (directly) benefited by the decision not to instantiate a bad life. So there is *an* asymmetry between coming into existence and going out of existence: with respect to death, someone is (directly) affected no matter what we decide to do, whereas whether or not someone is (directly) affected by our decisions concerning birth depends on what we decide to do. Nonetheless, Heyd's response leaves open the possibility that genethical judgements concerning people who *have been* (or will be) born are coherent, for in such cases there is a concrete subject to which harms and benefits can be ascribed. If one can be harmed or benefited by going out of existence then one can also be harmed or benefited by being created. But to say this is to depart from the no-faults view.

Heyd's second putative contrast between coming into existence and going out of existence invokes a desire-based account of the badness of death.

---

[6] Ibid. 123.

[Categorical] desires make us not only wish to go on living (not to commit suicide), but also to be happy that we did not die two years ago. But they cannot make us happy to have been born at all, since had we not been born there would not have been any such categorical desires.[7]

We can afford to ignore objections to the claim that the harm of death can be accounted for by appeal to frustrated desire, for Heyd's argument fails even if we assume a desire-based account of death's badness. If frustrated desire is able to explain death's badness then it can also explain that of birth. It is true that I wouldn't have had any categorical desires had I not been born, but it is also true that I wouldn't have had any categorical desires now had I died two years ago. Heyd seems to confuse the claim that an actual person might wish to not have been born with the claim that a non-actual person might have had wishes.[8] The latter claim is indeed incoherent, but the former claim is not. If it is coherent to prefer one possible future over another on account of the fact that in the former fewer of one's categorical desires are left unsatisfied, then it is also coherent to regret that the actual world is one in which one has many unsatisfied categorical desires (and few satisfied ones), rather than a world in which one doesn't (and didn't) exist and thus has no unsatisfied categorical desires (or, of course, satisfied ones).

Rather than tackle the no-faults model of genethicism 'head-on', I have instead argued against it by suggesting that no-faults gen-ethicists are committed to an Epicurean view of death. Epicureans, no doubt, will be nonplussed by this result, but true Epicureans are few on the ground. Coupled with its intrinsic counter-intuitive-ness, it seems to me that this result gives us reason to look elsewhere for an acceptable genethical model.

<hr />

[7] See Heyd, 1992.
[8] See Holtug, 2001.

III

Unlike no-faults genethicists, dual-benchmark genethicists allow that individuals can be harmed and benefited by coming into existence. Dual-benchmark genethicists also accept that it can be reasonable for a person doomed to a truly miserable life to regret having been born and for a person blessed with a happy life to celebrate their having come into existence. The dual-benchmark theorist departs from the proponent of the no-faults model in holding that there is a 'life worth living' benchmark. Roughly speaking, it is this benchmark that determines both whether or not it is pro tanto rational for the person in question to regret having come into existence and whether it was pro tanto permissible for the person in question to have been brought into existence.

In principle, there are two ways of being a dual-benchmark theorist. On the one hand, one could hold that the life-worth-starting threshold is lower than the life-worth-continuing threshold. Although this version of the view is coherent, it is deeply implausible. To the best of my knowledge, dual-benchmark theorists are united in insisting that the life-worth-starting benchmark is *higher* than the life-worth-continuing benchmark. (As we will see, some dual-benchmark theorists hold that the life-worth-starting benchmark is so high as to be practically unobtainable.)

Here is Benatar's statement of the dual-benchmark position (which he endorses):

The judgment that a disability is so bad that it makes life not worth continuing is usually made at a much higher threshold than the judgment that a disability is sufficiently bad to make life not worth beginning. That is to say, if a life is not worth continuing, *a fortiori* it is not worth beginning. It does not follow, however, that if a life is worth continuing that it is worth beginning or that if it is not worth beginning that it would not be worth continuing. For instance, while most people think that living life without a limb does not make life so bad that it is worth ending, most (of the same) people also think that it is better not to bring into

existence somebody who will lack a limb. We require stronger justification for ending a life than for not starting one.[9]

The dual-benchmark view has some intuitive plausibility. Although one could certainly take issue with the details of Benatar's
discussion (see below), his general point is well taken: the judgement that a disability is so bad that it makes life not worth
continuing *is* usually made at a much higher threshold than the
judgement that a disability is sufficiently bad to make life not worth
beginning.[10]

   But for all its intuitive plausibility the dual-benchmark approach
struggles to find adequate theoretical grounding, and common
attempts to ground the 'life-worth-starting' benchmark run the
risk of undermining the intuitive appeal of the model. Consider
the kinds of answers that dual-benchmark theorists typically give to
the question of where the 'life-worth-starting' benchmark ought to
be located.

Since we ought to try to provide every child with at least a normal
opportunity for a good life, and since we do not harm possible people if
we prevent them from existing, we ought to try to prevent the birth of
those with a significant risk of living worse than normal lives.[11]

I assume . . . that there is a strong moral obligation to prevent preventable
harm and suffering and that this obligation applies equally to curing disease
and injury and to preventing the avoidable creation of people who will
have disease or injury.[12]

These claims are startling. Purdy appeals to an unanalysed notion of
normality. Depending on exactly how this notion is cashed out, her
comments may well imply that a significant number of the world's
children should not have been brought into existence. Harris's
remarks lead in the same direction, for most of us will meet with

---

[9] Benatar, 2000: 176–7.
[10] For other genethical discussions that are sympathetic to the dual-benchmark approach,
see Peters, 1989; Cohen, 1997; Harman, 2004; Archard, 2004.
[11] Purdy, 1995: 302.
[12] Harris, 2000: 31.

some form of disease or injury during our lives. Dual-benchmark accounts are motivated by the common-sense intuition that it can be wrong to create someone with a severe handicap, but in their attempt to preserve this intuition they run the danger of flouting what is arguably an equally (if not more) robust intuition, namely, that the vast majority of children are *not* wronged by being brought into existence.

Some dual-benchmark theorists are quite happy to reject this intuition. As we will see, David Benatar holds that no life that contains any pain meets the 'life-worth-starting' threshold. Few dual-benchmark theorists will want to follow Benatar's lead, but those who want to set the life-worth-starting threshold lower—that is, at a point that most of us might actually meet—need to motivate their position. Purdy states that the interest we have in being free from disease or special limitation 'is sufficiently compelling in some cases to justify the judgment that reproducing would be wrong'.[13] But *when* are such interests 'sufficiently compelling', and what makes them sufficiently compelling in those cases and not others?

The dual-benchmark theorist might be tempted to appeal to species norms in setting the life-worth-starting benchmark, but it seems to me that this temptation should be resisted. Species norms change over time; certainly average levels of human well-being have increased significantly over the centuries. Relational properties such as 'being above (or below) the norm of well-being for one's species' might have an indirect bearing on genethical issues, for one's level of well-being is not unrelated to one's conception of how well one is doing relative to certain norms, but it seems implausible to suppose that they should play a direct role in determining whether or not one has been wronged by being brought into existence.

It might be argued that the parity account fares no better in providing a motivated account of where to locate the life-worth-

---

[13] Purdy, 1995: 307.

living benchmark. Not so. Although the parity account is not committed to any particular conception of where to draw the life-worth-starting benchmark, she can appeal to the sorts of reasons we invoke in evaluating the rationality of suicide or euthanasia—roughly, a life is worth living (starting or continuing) if there is reason to think that its goods will defeat its harms. We might call this the baseline (or neutrality) intuition. Obviously, fleshing this thought out would require an account of goods and harms, not to mention an account of how goods might defeat (or outweigh, counterbalance) harms. My point here is simply that the parity theorist has a principled account of where to place the life-worth-starting benchmark, even if developing that account requires a great deal of work.[14]

IV

Notwithstanding the problems facing the dual-benchmark theorist in locating the life-worth-starting benchmark, there is something to the thought that there is a gap between the kinds of lives that are worth starting and those that are worth continuing. As Benatar points out, there are people who we are inclined to regard as having been wrongly brought into existence, but we do not think that they would be better off dead. Call this the *marginal-life intuition*—'marginal' on account of the fact that it suggests that there is a margin (or 'gap') between the life-worth-starting and the life-worth-continuing benchmarks. The marginal-life *argument* builds on the marginal-life intuition by arguing that the dual-benchmark model

---

[14] Although the parity thesis and the baseline intuition hang together very nicely, the proponent of the parity account is not committed to endorsing the baseline intuition. A parity theorist could reject the idea that the life-worth-starting/continuing benchmark should be set at the level of neutral well-being, and hold that the only kinds of lives that are worth starting and continuing are ones in which life's goods *exceed* its bads. I'm not myself much drawn to this view, but perhaps it is defensible.

must be adopted on the grounds that it alone can account for and justify the marginal-life intuition.

Although I am inclined to think that there is something to the marginal-life intuition, I doubt that it is as robust as proponents of the dual-benchmark account have assumed. There is certainly some variability in our third-person genethical intuitions. While some people share Benatar's view that it is wrong to knowingly create a person who will lack a limb, others do not. Similarly, although some people think that it is wrong to knowingly bring a deaf child into existence, others regard such an act as ethically unproblematic. Not only do people differ in their views of supposedly marginal-life cases, it is relatively easy to shift people's responses to such cases by altering the contextual frame within which they are presented. (Would the deliberate creation of a person without a limb be wrong in a world in which *everyone* lacked a limb?)

Further, there is good reason to suspect that the marginal-life intuition is easily confused with other intuitions—intuitions that are not inconsistent with the parity model. In some situations, potential procreators are confronted by the need to choose between one of two potential persons, A and B. Now, where A is thought to be more likely to have a higher level of well-being than B, many have the intuition that the potential procreator ought to create A rather than B.[15] Perhaps we confuse the thought that B has a marginal life—that is, a life not worth starting—with the thought that S should have created A rather than B. But these are two quite different thoughts, and the latter does not entail the former. Another intuition with which the marginal-life intuition might be confused is that someone might be *unfortunate* to have been born with a certain condition. This intuition is also consistent with the parity model. The parity theorist denies that someone born without a limb has been *wronged* by having been brought into existence, but he need not deny that she is *unfortunate* to have been born without a limb. I suspect that in general we regard those born without a

---

[15] See Parfit, 1984; Savulescu, 2001; for a contrary view, see Belshaw, 2003.

limb as unfortunate to have been so born, and not—as Benatar suggests—as unfortunate to have been born at all. Perhaps the marginal-life intuition does not run as deep as dual-benchmark theorists suggest.

More importantly, *third-person* marginal-life judgements are not reflected in *first-person* marginal-life judgements. Consider the very example that Benatar uses: it is better not to bring into existence somebody who will lack a limb. Whatever intuitive support this claim might have, I strongly suspect that it has less intuitive support than the claim that someone born without a limb should regret having been born. Indeed, I suspect that most of us think that, *ceteris paribus*, it is unreasonable for those born without limbs to regret having been born. But if cases that generate third-person marginal-life intuitions do not also generate first-person marginal-life intuitions then the dual-benchmark theorist is faced with a problem, for it is highly plausible to suppose that first-person and third-person genethical judgements ought to be aligned. I have suggested that our third-person marginal-life intuitions might not be as strong or robust as dual-benchmark theorists suggest, but the conflict between them and our first-person genethical intuitions gives us reason to downgrade their force even further.

Proponents of the marginal-life argument might respond by arguing that we ought to resolve any conflict between our genethical intuitions by revising our *first-person* intuitions rather than our *third-person* intuitions. Benatar himself holds that we should *all* regret having been born, for we are all engaged in mass deception as to how wonderful things are for us.[16] I think that Benatar's view deserves serious consideration, but I lack the space to engage with it here. Suffice it to say that, although I am open to the possibility that we are often wrong about how well things are going for us, I find it difficult to believe that we are as fundamentally mistaken as Benatar's position requires. But perhaps the real issue here is that once we have reached this stage it is clear that the

---

[16] See Benatar, 2006: ch. 3.

marginal-life argument is no longer an argument from intuition but in fact rests on highly counter-intuitive claims.

Are there *any* cases that generate a reasonable first-person marginal-life intuition? Perhaps. Saul Smilansky considers a concentration camp survivor who, reflecting upon his life near its end, may feel that it was worthwhile. 'He might resent anyone implying otherwise. But when remembering the awful years of the war, his physical and psychological suffering, the loss of his first wife and child, and all the other relatives and friends, he may also think that having been spared the suffering, in not having been born, might have been preferable.'[17] What might this individual mean by the thought that his life 'has been worthwhile'? He could mean that he has made the best of it that he could. That seems plausible, but it would not generate a first-person marginal-life intuition, for that thought is consistent with the wish to never have been born. He could also mean that a particular segment of his life—for example, that which he now enjoys—has been good. That thought is also plausible, but it doesn't generate a first-person marginal-life intuition either. The only interpretation of this case that would involve a marginal-life intuition is one on which he both endorses his life as a whole and wishes that he had never been born. I find it difficult to understand how these attitudes could be consistently held. On reflection the marginal-life gap is a lot more tenuous than it might appear to be on first sight.[18]

---

[17] Smilansky, 1997: 243.

[18] Kamm (1993: 42, 64) points out that death is an insult to an existing entity—it is a manifestation of a person's vulnerability. Total non-existence, on the other hand, is not an insult, for it occurs to no actual entity. This, she suggests, might make it comprehensible why someone might prefer never having come into existence to even a good mortal life. One might regard the insult of death—independently of what it deprives one of—as an intrinsic bad that is best avoided if possible. The attitude that Kamm has outlined does not seem to be what Smilansky has in mind, but that does not detract from its interest. I myself am not convinced that the insult factor of death should be given much weight in this context, but perhaps it should not be dismissed.

V

I turn now to theoretical arguments in favour of the dual-benchmark view. Unlike the argument from marginal lives, these arguments support extreme versions of the dual-benchmark position according to which procreation is generally—if not universally—morally problematic.

I begin with Shiffrin's position.[19] Shiffrin argues that procreation is not a morally straightforward activity, but one that faces 'difficult justificatory hurdles'. In theory, she holds, *all* children have causes of action for wrongful life suits. Shiffrin's argument turns on the claim that it is impermissible to harm someone without their consent, even when the action that causes the harm brings about benefits that can be expected to outweigh the harms it causes. Since even the best of lives involves serious burdens, harms and risks, and since one cannot secure a person's consent before bringing them into existence, it follows that procreation is almost always morally problematic and procreators may be justifiably held responsible for the procreative harm that they cause. In every case, Shiffrin claims, voluntary procreation 'involves a person imposing a risk upon another where the imposition is not necessitated by the need to avert greater harm'.[20]

Shiffrin's argument is primarily addressed to 'prospective genethics', and it is less clear what her view of 'retrospective genethics' is (or should be). Shiffrin does *not* argue that most of us should regret having been born—indeed, the thrust of her argument is that one can be wronged by an event even when one has no cause to regret it. One might think that this in itself is problematic, but I'll leave that point aside here; instead, I want to focus on Shiffrin's rejection of parity between third-person starting-life and ending-life decisions.[21]

---

[19] Shiffrin. 1999.

[20] Ibid. 139.

[21] Shiffrin takes no position on how first-person genethical attitudes ought to relate to third-person genethical attitudes, or indeed, on how first-person genethical attitudes ought to relate to first-person attitudes to death.

Suppose that you are deliberating about whether or not to preserve the life of a patient who is temporarily comatose. The patient is suffering a life-threatening illness, but if treated can be expected to make a full recovery. It seems clear that in such a case it is not only permissible to save the patient's life but obligatory. Prima facie, however, Shiffrin's position would seem to entail that we ought to let the patient die. After all, saving the patient's life exposes her to serious future harms and burdens that she would otherwise avoid, and such harms are unconsented. Call this the *comatose patient* case.

Shiffrin might respond by arguing that although saving the patient's life exposes her to future harms (sickness, suffering, loneliness, etc.), it also saves her from a greater harm, namely death. But on what grounds can Shiffrin argue that death is a harm? (Indeed, on what grounds can she argue that killing someone without their consent is wrong, given that it prevents unconsented harms?) Shiffrin does not provide a full answer to this question, but she does suggest that death is bad because it interferes with the exercise of agency. 'By constraining the duration and possible contents of the person's life, [death] forces a particular end to the person— making her with respect to that significant aspect of her life merely passive.'[22]

At best, this account of death's badness might account for our intuitions concerning the deaths of autonomous, self-conscious individuals. It is harder to see how it might account for the badness of the death of infants, the severely mentally retarded, the senile, and others who lack full agency over their own lives. Yet the fact that a comatose patient might happen to be a young child seems not to change our intuitions concerning what we ought to do. We ought to save the comatose patient's life, even if she is only a week old. And in saving her life we impose (or at least allow) roughly the same amount of unconsented harm that was imposed on the child by creating her.

[22] Ibid. 124.

Taking another tack, Shiffrin might supplement her account of the wrongness of death by appeal to the notion of *desert*. Perhaps death—even the death of infants—is bad because it robs its victim of the goods of life that they deserve. The infant has made an 'investment' in her life, and depriving her of a 'return' on that investment would constitute a harm to her. By contrast, potential individuals have made no investment in their life and are thus not owed anything.

There is much that is problematic about the idea that desert might ground the badness of infant death, but I won't pursue those problems here.[23] Even if there are desert-based reasons for thinking that the infant is harmed by death, those reasons must be weighed against the fact that saving the infant's life exposes them to unconsented harms and burdens—'the fairly substantial amount of pain, suffering, difficulty, significant disappointment, distress, and significant loss that occur within the typical life'.[24] Surely *these* features of life are not deserved. It seems entirely possible that the (unconsented) harms that we expose the infant to by saving her life might outweigh the harm of death, especially given the fact that death is never avoided but only postponed. Suppose that the infant is now six months old, and saving her will give her another eighty or so years of life. If Shiffrin is to argue that saving the infant's life is obligatory, she must argue that death at six months is worse than death at eighty years, and worse in such a way as to balance the fact that saving the patient's life incurs eighty years of unconsented harms. There are a number of accounts of why death at six months of age is worse than death at eighty (other things being equal), but many of these accounts turns on the claim that it is a good thing to extend life, even when the subject in question faces significant unconsented harm. If such accounts are acceptable here it is unclear why a similar line of reasoning cannot be used to justify procreation:

---

[23] See McMahan, 2002: 168.
[24] Shiffrin, 1999: 137.

it is permissible to create life, even when doing so involves un-consented harms.

I suspect that the most plausible response that Shiffrin might make to the comatose patient objection is to invoke the notion of substituted judgement. Perhaps it is permissible to save the coma-tose patient's life because we think that were we in the comatose patient's position (albeit, of course, not comatose) we too would desire that our life be saved. But if it is permissible to employ substituted judgements here then there can be no objection to employing them in genethical contexts. Would-be parents can justify their decision to have a child on the grounds that were they (or some suitable idealization of them) in the child's position, they would consent to having been brought into existence.

VI

As already noted, David Benatar argues that being brought into existence is not a benefit but *always* a harm, and that each of us should regret having come into existence.[25] Benatar's argument for these claims turns on a putative asymmetry between pains and pleasures: whereas the absence of pain is itself good, the absence of pleasure is not bad (unless there is someone for whom this absence is a deprivation).

According to Benatar, in order to determine the relative advan-tages and disadvantages of coming into existence and never coming to be we need to compare (1) with (3) and (2) with (4): see Figure 2.1. When we do this, Benatar says, we discover that (3) is better than (1), but (2) is not better than (4): 'the pleasures of existence, although good, are not a real advantage over non-existence, be-cause the absence of pleasures is not bad'.[26] All things considered, non-existence is preferable to existence because there is nothing

---

[25] See Benatar, 2000, 2006.
[26] Benatar, 1997: 348.

World A X exists	World B X never exists
1) Presence of Pain (Bad)	3) Absence of Pain (Good)
2) Presence of Pleasure (Good)	4) Absence of Pleasure (Not-Bad)

Figure 2.1 Benatar's matrix

bad about never coming into existence but there is (invariably) something bad about coming into existence.[27] Let us call this *Benatar's asymmetry*.

There are several puzzling features about this matrix. First, there is something intuitively odd about describing worlds in which S does not exist as 'good for S'. It is difficult to see how anything could be good (or bad, for that matter) for someone in worlds in which they don't exist. (This, of course, is a point that no-faults theorists such as Heyd are at pains to emphasize.) Further, even if worlds in which S doesn't exist are good for S, it doesn't follow that such worlds will be better for S than worlds in which S does exist. Goods and bads aggregate; generally speaking, a life with more goods is better than one with fewer goods. But if this is so, then we need to know how *much* 'pain' and 'pleasure' S has in *A* in order to know whether or not *A* is worse for S than *B* is. But perhaps the most pressing question concerns Benatar's asymmetry itself. Is it true?

Benatar defends it on the grounds that it provides the best explanation of the following four genethical intuitions.[28] Firstly,

---

[27] Benatar's view is closely akin to 'frustrationism', see Fehige, 1998: 508–43; Holtug, 2001. Frustrationists claim that the value of satisfying a preference equals that of not having it, i.e. it has zero value. By contrast, the frustration of a preference has negative value. On this conception of value, the best that one could possibly hope to get out of life would be to break even—which is the value equivalent to not having been born. But since even the best of lives involves some pain and frustration, one should expect that one will come out of life 'in the red', that is, with negative value. So it is almost certain that everyone is better off not having been born. Benatar differs from the frustrationist in taking the presence of pleasure to be good whereas the frustrationist views it as merely neutral.

[28] Benatar, 2006: 31–6; see also p. 203.

although there is a duty to avoid bringing suffering people into existence there is no duty to bring happy people into being.[29] Secondly, 'whereas it is strange (if not incoherent) to give as a reason for having a child that the child one has will thereby be benefited, it is not strange to cite a potential child's interests as a basis for avoiding bringing a child into existence'.[30] Thirdly, bringing people into existence as well as failing to bring people into existence can be regretted, but only bringing people into existence can be regretted for the sake of the person whose existence was contingent on our decision.[31] Fourthly, whereas we are rightly sad for inhabitants of a foreign land whose lives are characterized by suffering, when we hear that some island is unpopulated we are not similarly sad for the happy people who, had they existed, would have populated this island.[32]

These four claims certainly have some intuitive grip on us, and the ability of Benatar's account to justify them would indeed be a mark in its favour. But these intuitions are by no means our only genethical intuitions. We are also strongly committed to the claim that individuals with normal human lives—not to mention individuals with lives that are vastly superior to the average human life— are not harmed by being created. We would be in something of a genethical pickle were it to turn out that these intuitions are not reconcilable with each other, but it's not obvious that the best way to extricate ourselves from that pickle is to embrace Benatar's asymmetry. As an alternative, we could reject the four genethical intuitions that Benatar appeals to, or even give up on genethical intuition altogether. Of course, each of these moves comes at some cost, but it is not clear that this cost would be higher than that which Benatar's solution incurs. Benatar himself seems to think that his view is not counter-intuitive—'there is nothing implausible either in the view that coming into existence is always a harm or

---

[29] Ibid. 32.
[30] Ibid. 34.
[31] Ibid.
[32] Ibid. 35.

in the view that we ought not to have children'[33]—but I suspect that the vast majority would disagree with him on that point. Evaluating the weight of intuition is a tricky business, but I am not convinced that the combined weight of the four intuitions that Benatar invokes in support of his view exceeds that of the genethical intuitions that he rejects.[34]

Let us return to Benatar's asymmetry, and the question of whether it provides the best explanation of the four intuitions that he presents. Clearly, the answer to this question depends on the precise content of the intuitions in question. Let us begin with the first intuition. Is it the case that there is a duty to avoid creating suffering people but no duty to create happy people? In large part that depends on just what one means by 'suffering people'. Almost no one thinks that we have a duty to avoid creating people who will experience *some* suffering, but if a 'suffering person' is someone whose entire life on balance involves more pain (broadly construed) than pleasure (broadly construed) then he is right: we do have a strong pre-theoretical commitment to the view that there is a duty to avoid bringing such people into existence. And, equally, we have a strong (albeit, perhaps, less strong) commitment to the view that there is no duty to bring happy people into being. But I'm not convinced that Benatar's asymmetry provides the best explanation of this intuition. An even better explanation would appeal to an asymmetry between good and bad *lives* rather than to an asymmetry between good and bad *experiences*. The best explanation of our intuition is simply that we think it is good to avoid a miserable life but not bad to miss out on a good life. This explanation

[33] Benatar, 2006: 207.

[34] At various points in *Better Never to Have Been* Benatar seeks to downplay the force of intuition. 'Intuitions are often profoundly unreliable, the product of mere prejudice. Views that are taken to be deeply counter-intuitive in one time and place are often taken to be obviously true in another' (p. 203). No doubt there is much truth in all of this, but it doesn't follow that genethical intuitions have no evidential force at all. Indeed, Benatar's own case for the dual-benchmark view rests heavily on the marginal-life intuition, not to mention the four intuitions just mentioned.

accounts for our intuitions, and it does so without the counter-intuitive consequences of Benatar's view.

The second claim that Benatar invokes to support his account is: 'whereas it is strange (if not incoherent) to give as a reason for having a child that the child one has will thereby be benefited, it is not strange to cite a potential child's interests as a basis for avoiding bringing a child into existence'.[35] Again, we do endorse this judgement, but only up to a point. It doesn't seem strange to cite a potential child's *overall* interests or well-being as a basis for avoiding bringing it into existence; in particular, it doesn't seem strange to think that if the potential child's (expected) pain would be such as to overwhelm its (expected) pleasures, then one should not bring it into existence. But it *does* seem strange to cite a potential child's expected pains as a basis for avoiding bringing it into existence *without at the same time* being prepared to cite its expected pleasures as a basis for bringing it into existence. Here too our common-sensical genethical judgements seem to be grounded in the expected quality of the target's overall life, not in some disembodied calculus involving individual pleasures and pains.

Benatar's third claim is this: 'bringing people into existence as well as failing to bring people into existence can be regretted, but only bringing people into existence can be regretted for the sake of the person whose existence was contingent on our decision'.[36] Again, this judgement does seem to be one that we share, but in order to explain it we need invoke only an asymmetry between good and bad *lives*: whereas we regret having brought bad lives into existence, we do not regret not having brought good lives into existence. There is an asymmetry here, but it is not one that supports Benatar's asymmetry. The kinds of lives that we regret having brought into existence are not those of normal human beings, but those in which the goods of life are outweighed by its bads.

[35] Ibid. 34.
[36] Ibid.

What about the fourth judgement? Here too the objects of our evaluation appear to be entire lives. We are sad for inhabitants of foreign lands whose lives are so characterized by suffering that we think that they would be better off dead, and we are happy—or at least not sad—for inhabitants of foreign lands whose lives are such that we do not think that they would be better off dead.

The moral of the foregoing is simple: there *is* an asymmetry in our genethical judgements, but we do violence to that asymmetry if we attempt to explain it in terms of pains and pleasures (or bads and goods) in isolation. The best systematization of these four judgements is that there is a deep asymmetry between good lives and bad lives.

Benatar might object that we haven't really *explained* these four genethical judgements by invoking an asymmetry between good and bad lives but have simply redescribed them. He might argue that we need to invoke a further, deeper asymmetry—his asymmetry—between events or states in order to explain my asymmetry (between lives). I'm not persuaded. Not only would taking this extra step add nothing to what we already have, but it would incur costs of its own. It adds nothing, for Benatar provides no explanation of his asymmetry. He has no story to tell as to how it could be a good thing for S to avoid pains by failing to exist without it also being a bad thing for S to avoid pleasures by failing to exist. And it incurs additional costs, for it is at odds with our judgement that we do not harm normal people by bringing them into existence. Better, I think, to treat the asymmetry between good lives and bad lives as brute.

VII

Although Benatar urges us not to procreate, he does not urge us to commit suicide or to refrain from offering life-saving treatment to those in need of it. I find this fact puzzling. If one could have benefited by not having being born on account of the pain that one avoids, so too one can benefit from an early death on account of the pain that one avoids.

In response, Benatar claims that his point is not that 'it is better never to exist because one thereby avoids pains, but that it is better never to exist because one avoids pains *without cost*. The same is not true of death. Whereas death does spare one all future pains, it does involve a cost' (personal communication). I certainly agree that death does exact a price—it robs one of the goods that one would have enjoyed had one continued to exist.[37] But there is also a sense in which non-existence comes at a cost—namely, the goods that one would have enjoyed had one come into existence. Of course, *strictly speaking*, this cost is not incurred by anyone, for only the existent can be robbed. But, if we are speaking strictly, then we must also insist that only the existent can *benefit* from having dodged disaster. Insisting on strict speech threatens to undercut the very asymmetry that Benatar is at pains to defend.

Perhaps these points are most fully appreciated by considering death from the first-person perspective. Let us suppose that you are contemplating suicide, and that other parties will not be greatly affected by your decision. In deliberating about whether or not to commit suicide, it may seem reasonable to adopt a genethical stance towards the remainder of your life. Call the subject of this life-segment 'future-you'. You could bring future-you into being by deciding not to commit suicide, or you could make it the case that future-you never exists by committing suicide. How should you decide? From a certain perspective, it seems reasonable to decide on the basis of what quality of life future-you can be expected to enjoy: if it is good, then deciding in favour of continued existence may be reasonable, if it is bad, then deciding in favour of suicide may be unreasonable. Thinking of oneself as faced with decisions about whether or not to allow a future self to come into existence brings to the surface deep points of contact between coming into existence and staying in existence. Our lives are not given once and for

[37] F. Feldman, 1992; McMahan, 2002.

all. The question of whether to stay in existence always contains within itself a question about whether to bring 'the rest of oneself' into existence.

In thinking about whether or not to remain in existence it seems reasonable to adopt a form of substituted judgement: one adopts the perspective of one's future self. But if this is reasonable, why is it not also reasonable to adopt such a perspective with respect to coming into existence? If, in adopting the perspective of the person who would be brought into existence as the result of the relevant deliberation, one decides that the expected goods outweigh the expected bads, then (ceteris paribus) procreation is permissible; if not, then it is not permissible.

VIII

Let me turn finally to the parity account. The basic idea behind the approach is encapsulated in Bernard Williams's claim that 'what [resenting one's existence] requires is that the person should prefer not to have existed, and I take it that this implies thinking that his or her life is not worth living'.[38] 'Implies' might be too strong a term here, but the parity account is built on the idea that there are internal constraints between the ethics of starting lives and the ethics of continuing them. These constraints apply not merely to one's own life but to lives in general: if one thinks that life could never be so bad as to be not worth continuing, then one should also think that life could never be so bad as to be not worth starting, and vice versa. We can—and should—employ intuitions concerning coming into existence to constrain our views about going out of existence and vice versa.

The parity model is grounded in the thought that judgements about coming into existence and judgements about going out of existence ought to be responsive to the same features of the world—namely, the value that the life in question would have to

---

[38] Williams, 1995: 227.

its subject. If living a life is of no value to its subject then it is pro tanto pointless to begin it and pointless to maintain it. But if the living of a life is (or at least has the potential to be) of benefit to its subject then, again pro tanto, there is some point in both beginning it and maintaining it.

Of course, there are differences between judgements that concern coming into existence and those that concern staying in existence. One difference is that the former concern the subject's *entire life*, whereas the latter typically focus only on certain *segments* of the subject's life—namely, those segments that the subject has not yet enjoyed. Overlooking this point can lead one astray. Consider again Smilansky's case of the concentration camp survivor—call him 'Carl'—whose life contained a period of grotesque suffering. Carl might have the view that his life as a whole was not worth living. Does parity entail that he would *now* be better off dead? Not at all, for Carl has survived the horrors of the concentration camp, and that period of his life that lies in front of him may well be worth living. Parity does *not* entail that if the value of an entire life is below the 'life worth living' threshold then at no point in the living of that life is it worth continuing. Parity says only that the kinds of conditions that make lives not worth creating are just the sorts of conditions that make lives not worth continuing, and it is obviously possible for a life to be characterized by such a condition during some of its temporal segments but not others.

A second difference between judgements that concern coming into existence and those which concern staying in existence lies in their respective intentional objects. Judgements of the latter kind have as their objects token lives—that is, concrete particulars. By contrast, judgements of the former kind take abstract entities as their intentional objects. These judgements are about the merits or otherwise of instantiating certain *kinds* of lives. Arguably, it is this difference that grounds that otherwise puzzling fact that although we have obligations to keep good lives in existence we do not have obligations to start good lives: the difference, of course, is that we have obligations to concrete particulars but not to abstract entities.

IX

My goal here has not been to provide a comprehensive treatment of genethics. Such a task is clearly beyond the means of a single chapter; indeed, I suspect that it is beyond the means of even a decent-sized volume. Rather, I have attempted to provide a framework for thinking about genethics. I have argued that our thinking about starting lives should be constrained by our thinking about ending lives, and vice versa. In the relevant sense, the 'life-worth-starting' benchmark coincides with the 'life-worth-continuing' benchmark, for each is but a manifestation of the 'life-worth-living' benchmark.

In closing, let me mention one of the many implications of this position. One of the many worries that courts have expressed about wrongful life cases is that a positive verdict would commit the court to the view that the plaintiff not only ought not to have been brought into existence, but would now be better off dead. Although the worry as stated is groundless, there is something both true and important to it. The reason the conclusion does not strictly follow is that the plaintiff's current quality of life (and, indeed, that which they might be expected to enjoy in the future) might differ in important respects from the quality of their life as a whole. And—as we have just seen—it is possible for the quality of the person's life to improve such that they currently have a life that is worth living, even though their life as a whole is of no benefit to them. Nonetheless, the thought behind the worry is basically sound: the kinds of conditions that prevent life from being worth starting are just those that prevent it from being worth continuing.[39]

[39] Thanks to David Archard, David Benatar, Avery Kolers, and Neil Levy for very helpful comments on earlier drafts of this chapter. Earlier versions were presented to the philosophy departments at the University of Louisville, Charles Sturt University (Wagga Wagga), University College Cork, and the University of Hull. I am grateful to the audiences on those occasions for their comments.

3

An Ordinary Chance of a Desirable Existence

MICHAEL PARKER

> Any philosopher who wants to keep his contact with man-
> kind should pervert his own system in advance to see how it
> will really look a few decades after adoption.[1]

The decision to have a child is one of the most morally significant things we do.[2] Recent advances in reproductive medicine have dramatically increased the moral complexity of reproductive deci-sion-making. Whereas prior to such advances the main moral questions for potential parents would have required consideration of the features of the social, economic, and physical environment into which the child would be born, recent developments in reproductive medicine mean that such questions increasingly in-clude consideration of the future child's biological characteristics. The number and complexity of such choices is likely to increase in the future. This chapter investigates the obligations people thinking of becoming parents through the use of new reproductive technol-ogies have with respect to the life they are about to create.

---

[1] Bellow, 1965: 319.
[2] J. S. Mill, *On Liberty* (1859), in Mill, 1993: 177.

In Praise of Experiments of Living

John Stuart Mill is frequently called upon by those who wish to argue for a *laissez-faire* approach to the introduction and regulation of new biotechnologies. In so doing, they tend to draw upon a strongly libertarian interpretation of Mill emphasizing the importance of what has come to be known as his 'harm principle'. Following Mill, they argue that the only grounds upon which the use of reproductive technologies can justifiably be overruled is to prevent harm.[3]

... the sole end for which mankind are warranted, individually or collectively, in interfering with the liberty of action of any of their number, is self-protection. ... the only purpose for which power can rightfully exercised over any member of a civilized community, against his will, is to prevent harm to others.[4]

People who wish to use reproductive technologies such as genetic testing or preimplantation genetic diagnosis should, it is argued, be free to do so even if others disapprove, or would not use them themselves, as long as their so doing does not cause significant harm to others.

The use of the harm principle to justify a libertarian approach to the availability and use of reproductive technologies tends to be complemented by the use of another key Millian concept, that of 'experiments of living'.[5] For Mill, the importance of such experiments is instrumental, for they constitute the conditions most conducive to 'individual and social progress'.[6]

As it is useful that while mankind are imperfect there should be different opinions, so is it that there should be different experiments of living: that free scope should be given to varieties of character, short of injury to

---

[3] Such arguments are also, for obvious reasons, associated with claims that there is no evidence that the use of such technologies present real harms.

[4] Mill, 1993: 78.

[5] Ibid. 124.

[6] Ibid.

others; and that the worth of different modes of life should be proved practically, when anyone thinks fit to try them.[7]

Experiments of living are important for Mill because he believes that the 'worth of different modes of life should be proved practically'[8] and the 'fullest and freest comparison of opposite opinions [is] of value, because mankind are not infallible; . . . [and] their truths, for the most part [are] only half-truths'.[9] While for Mill, the importance of experiments of living, and hence also of liberty is tied to the value of individual and social progress, in the work of libertarians the commitment to progress as a justification for reproductive freedom is rarely explicit even if such considerations are seldom far from the surface.

From a young age, Mill placed particular emphasis on the importance of liberty in sexual and reproductive matters.[10] In this regard his arguments about sex and reproduction do indeed prefigure contemporary liberal approaches to reproductive ethics. Nevertheless, Mill's reproductive ethics is not libertarian in the way that the readings of many bioethicists would suggest. For while reproduction is an area of life in which Mill clearly considers liberty to be important, it is also singled out by him as a domain in which other moral principles, and the evidence provided by previous experiments of living, have the potential to come into conflict with and indeed override considerations of liberty.

It is not in the matter of education only that misplaced notions of liberty prevent moral obligations on the part of parents from being recognised, and legal obligations from being imposed, where there are strongest grounds for the former always, and in many cases for the later also. The fact itself, of causing the existence of a human being, is one of the most responsible actions in the range of human life which may be either a curse

---

[7] Ibid.
[8] Ibid.
[9] Ibid.
[10] Reeves, 2007: 1.

or a blessing—unless the being upon whom it is be bestowed will have at least the ordinary chances of a desirable existence, is a crime against that being.[11]

Mill's emphasis here on the importance of an 'ordinary chance of a desirable existence' suggests that the 'results' of previous experiments of living and the current state of our knowledge about the kinds of things that make a life go well or badly are of moral significance and have the potential to generate important parental obligations of reproductive beneficence.[12] For Mill moreover, the state can on occasion be justified in interfering in reproductive choice to ensure the conditions for a desirable existence,

The laws which, in many countries on the Continent, forbid marriage unless the parties can show that they have the means of supporting a family, do not exceed the legitimate powers of the State: and whether such laws be expedient or not (a question mainly dependent on local circumstances and feelings), they are not objectionable as violations of liberty.[13]

It is apparent that for Mill reproduction is a morally significant area of life in which there are tensions between liberty and beneficence, between the parents' liberty to pursue experiments of living on the one hand and their obligations to take account of what is already known—from previous experiments and experience—on the other to secure for their child the ordinary chance of a desirable existence. While Mill places significant weight on obligations of reproductive beneficence however, his commitment to liberty means that cases justifying the use of state intervention are going to be limited. It is clear that, for Mill, parents do not have an obligation to provide the child with an ideal childhood. Their obligations are limited to ensuring the 'ordinary chance of a desirable existence'. Beyond

---

[11] Mill, 1993: 177.

[12] I use the concept of 'reproductive beneficence' here to refer to Mill's view that in their reproductive decision-making potential parents have obligations of beneficence in relation to the lives of the children who will result from their reproductive choices.

[13] Ibid. 177–8.

this parents should be free of both external interference, and of personal moral obligations of beneficence.

The Problem

Developments in reproductive technology mean that, whereas for Mill the tensions between liberty and beneficence concern the nature of the social, economic, and physical environment into which the child is to be born and raised, in contemporary discussions such concerns are further complicated by the possibility of selecting the biological characteristics of the child.[14] The development of *in vitro* fertilization (IVF) combined with preimplantation genetic diagnosis (PGD), means that it has become possible to select from amongst a set of embryos produced through IVF for the biological characteristics present in the available embryos. What this means is that potential parents with access to such technologies have the option to assess the implications of the genetic make-up of different embryos for the lives of the children who would be produced through their implantation and to decide in each case whether or not implantation should go ahead. The development and potential for widespread availability of such technologies means that the issues falling under the scope of reproductive ethics have been transformed dramatically in the years since 1859 when Mill published *On Liberty*.[15] Despite this, Mill's consideration of the important tensions between reproductive liberty and reproductive beneficence in the light of empirical evidence about what makes lives go well foreshadows much debate in contemporary reproductive ethics.

Consider the following anonymized case:

---

[14] Buchanan *et al.*, 2000.

[15] It is important to note here that by its very nature the uptake of PGD, which requires women to go through all the procedures associated with IVF, is to some extent self-limiting. It is unlikely that a large proportion of the population is going to be interested in undergoing the required procedures in order to select for anything but the most serious of conditions.

A woman is going through IVF because she wants to have a child but is infertile. Unrelated to the cause of her infertility, the woman is an unaffected carrier of X-linked spondyloepiphyseal dysplasia tarda (SED). As a carrier, and because the condition is X-linked, she has equal 1 in 4 chances of: an affected son; an unaffected son; a carrier daughter; and a non-carrier daughter. She is considering whether she should use PGD to test the embryos for SED and only implant unaffected or non-carrier embryos. Does she have a moral duty to use PGD to choose the 'best possible child'? Because it is X-linked, SED only affects males. At birth, affected boys are of normal length and proportions and reach normal motor and cognitive milestones. However, between 5 and 12 years of age their linear growth is retarded with the result that their final adult height is usually between 4'10" and 5'6". They have a short trunk and barrel shaped chest. Affected men tend to get some back and joint pain, and some osteoarthritis and restricted joint movement. In some, but not all, cases, early hip replacement (e.g. in 30s) and pain management is required. In majority of cases however care is mostly 'support' and advice to avoid certain occupations e.g. those that involve stress on the spine. They have normal intelligence and life expectancy.

Such cases present a number of recognizable tensions between reproductive beneficence and reproductive liberty. Do potential parents such as the woman in this case have an obligation to use PGD to select a child free of the disease? To what extent should they be free to refuse to do so, or even, were they so to decide, to implant an embryo that would develop into a child who would be affected by the condition? To what extent should these choices be limited by either policy or regulation? I shall return to this particular case later in this chapter, but first I want to discuss another well-known case, which for some commentators tested reproductive liberty and beneficence to their limits.

In 2001, Sharon Duchesneau and Candy McCullough, a deaf lesbian couple living in Washington, DC, had their second child, Gauvin.[16] Like their first, Jehanne, he was born deaf. The women,

---

[16] Mundy, 2002.

who wanted to have a deaf child, conceived Gauvin through Artificial Insemination by Donor (AID), using sperm from a friend they knew to have five generations of inherited deafness in his family.[17] Initially they had approached a local sperm bank but were told that congenital deafness was one of the conditions that ruled out would-be donors. In an extended interview in the *Washington Post*, Sharon and Candy gave several reasons for their decision to have a deaf child.[18] They argued that the child would grow up to be a valued member of a real and supportive deaf community; deafness is an identity, not a medical affliction that needs to be fixed; they would be able to be better parents to a deaf child than to one who was hearing; the desire to have a deaf child is a natural outcome of the pride and self-acceptance many people have of being deaf; and, for this reason, while a hearing child would be a blessing, a deaf child would be a special blessing.

The concept of 'Deaf Culture' has been discussed extensively elsewhere.[19] Notwithstanding the intricacies of this academic and political debate however, Sharon and Candy seem to have had a more everyday kind of community in mind. For both women live close to Gallaudet University in Washington, the world's first liberal arts university for the deaf, where most of the staff are deaf. Most staff and students and their families live nearby creating, according to the *Washington Post*, something that might be called a deaf 'community' in the everyday sense of the word.[20]

Like the case of SED above, the reproductive choices made by Sharon and Candy raise a number of important moral questions. Is there a moral duty to have a 'healthy' child in situations where there is a choice?[21] If so, what is to count as 'healthy' and/or 'disabled' and who is to decide in any particular case?[22] What, if any, are the

---

[17] Wikler and Wikler, 1991.
[18] Mundy, 2002.
[19] Padden and Humphries, 2005.
[20] The website for Gallaudet University can be found at <http://www.gallaudet.edu/>.
[21] T. Shakespeare, 1998.
[22] Parens and Asch, 1999.

appropriate limits of reproductive freedom?[23] What are the appropriate relationships between personal morality, professional ethics, and regulation in reproductive decision-making?

In a paper discussing the ethical issues presented by this case and their implications for reproductive medicine more broadly Julian Savulescu proposes two principles of reproductive ethics.[24] He calls these principles, 'reproductive autonomy' and 'procreative beneficence'. Following John Robertson,[25] who uses the Millian term 'liberty' rather than autonomy, Savulescu argues that in their reproductive decision-making people should be 'free to do what others disapprove of or judge wrong, provided the exercise of freedom does not harm others'.[26] In justifying respect for reproductive autonomy, he draws upon and emphasizes the value of 'experiments of living'.

Procreative Beneficence

Whereas Mill requires of potential parents only that they ensure for their child, on the basis of the best available information, an ordinary chance of a desirable existence, Savulescu's principle of 'procreative beneficence', is much more demanding, requiring of potential parents that they choose, of the possible children available to them, those with the best opportunity of having the best life.[27] In relation to genetic testing for example, he argues that, 'Couples should employ genetic tests to have the child, of the possible children they could have, who will have the best opportunity of the best life.'[28] It is important to note that, like Derek Parfit[29] and

---

[23] Mitchie and Marteau, 1999.
[24] Savulescu, 2002.
[25] Robertson, 1994.
[26] Savulescu, 2002: 771; Parker, 2005.
[27] Savulescu, 2001.
[28] Savulescu, 2002: 771.
[29] Parfit, 1984.

John Robertson, Savulescu does not argue that choosing to have a child other than the one with the best opportunity of the best life is to harm that child.[30] A child who is born deaf is not harmed by his or her parents in cases such as the one above because no alternative, better, life is available to that child.[31] If Candy and Sharon had chosen to use sperm from a hearing donor, the resulting child would not have been the same child minus the deafness. It would be a different child. 'If the child has no way to be born or raised free of that harm, a person is not injuring the child by enabling her to be born in the circumstances of concern.'[32] For Savulescu potential parents have a duty to have the child with the best opportunity of the best life, not because to fail to do so would harm the child, but because they have a duty to bring about the best lives they can.

While the case of the deaf couple is unusual, it is an important case because practical ethical questions about the limits of autonomy and beneficence arise frequently in the day-to-day practice of reproductive medicine and these questions are confronted in particularly stark terms in this case offering the potential for a discussion of the demands of reproductive medicine and the limits of reproductive beneficence. To what extent should everyday reproductive decision-making be guided by Savulescu's principle? Is there a duty to have the child with the best opportunity of the best life and if so, what does this mean in situations like the one facing the woman who is a carrier of SED in the case I presented earlier? The cases above involving deafness and short stature are both ones which, at first glance, present a conflict between reproductive autonomy and procreative beneficence, that is, while respect for autonomy requires Sharon's choice to be respected, and for the woman who is a carrier of SED to be free to choose the

---

[30] This is an important point of divergence between Savulescu and Mill for whom arguments about 'non-identity' were unavailable.

[31] An exception is when the condition is so bad that it would be better not to have existed at all, but these situations will be rare.

[32] Robertson, 1994: 75.

embryo she wishes to implant, concerns about beneficence, for Savulescu, require the avoidance of deafness or short stature.

For Savulescu, by contrast with Mill, there can be no conflict between reproductive autonomy and reproductive beneficence where there is no person–affecting harm. This suggests that for Savulescu while reproductive autonomy means that it would be wrong for the women to be stopped from making the choices they wish to make, it would nevertheless (because of the principle of procreative beneficence) be morally wrong for them to choose to have a deaf or short-statured child when they could avoid this. They should choose, of the possible children available to them, the child who will start life with the best opportunity of having the best life, even though no one has the right to impose this choice on them. The choice to have a disabled child is wrong for Savulescu, as we have seen, not because it would harm the resulting child, but because it would bring about a worse life than could have been the case. As a consequence, Savulescu believes that these are choices to be made by potential parents themselves.

Problems with Savulescu's Principle of Procreative Beneficence

In what follows, I shall argue that while I agree that potential parents such as Sharon and the woman who is a carrier of SED have important obligations of beneficence when choosing between the bringing about of different possible lives, the concept of a duty to have the child with the best opportunity of the best life is not a coherent way to capture such obligations. The principle of 'procreative beneficence', where this is taken to imply a duty to have the child with the best opportunity of the best life, is underdetermining, paradoxical, and self-defeating.

(i) The principle of procreative beneficence is underdetermining

Moral principles require interpretation if they are to be applied in particular cases.[33] A minimum requirement for the meaningful application of Savulescu's principle of procreative beneficence is that it be capable of *ranking* possible lives as 'better' or 'worse',[34] not only in the sense that, say, a 'hearing' embryo will be more likely to grow into a child who can hear better than one that is 'deaf', but also in relation to concepts involved in the understanding of a life as the 'best possible life'. The key concepts requiring interpretation for the application of the principle in this second sense are complex. Not least complex among these is the concept of the 'best life' itself, which is meaningful only in relation to other similarly rich and complex concepts such as those of the 'good life', 'human flourishing', 'well-being', and of what it is that makes lives 'go well'. This is not to suggest that the significance of these concepts would need to be established before that of the 'best life' could be understood and used as the basis for interpretation, but to highlight rather the fact that any coherent use of the principle of procreative beneficence in ranking possible lives would unavoidably involve ranking the characteristics of, say, embryos, in relation to a particular cluster of complex, rich, and interdependent moral concepts.

This is not possible for two reasons. The first of these arises from the very fact that complex concepts and networks of concepts such as those of the 'good life', the 'best life', and 'human flourishing', are not reducible to simple 'elements' or constituent 'parts' which might be identified through the testing of embryos. There are a number of interrelated reasons for doubting the possibility of re-ducing the good life to simple elements of this kind. First, if we take a moment to consider our own lives, those of our friends and family, or those we have read about, such experience tells us that

---

[33] O'Neill, 1996.
[34] Broome, 1995.

it is extremely difficult in advance, and perhaps also even in retro-spect, to say with any authority what it is, or was, that makes (or made) a life go well. Is it true for example, that a life free of troubled interpersonal relationships, free of suffering, loneliness, or misun-derstanding is a better life, or even, taken as a whole, a *happier* life, than one in which experience of these to at least some degree has played a part?[35] Is it true to say that the good life is the life free of any illness, disease, or misfortune?[36] To ask these questions is not of course to suggest that nothing at all can be said about what makes a life go well or badly, nor is it to suggest that misfortune is a good thing. It is rather to reflect upon the fact that whilst it may be possible to delineate some conditions conducive to good lives, it is not going to be possible to relate the testable features of embryos in any useful or determinative sense to concepts as rich and complex as that of the 'good life', and thereby to rank possible lives as 'better' or 'worse'. This means that the concept of the 'opportunity of the best possible life' is inevitably underdetermining. Part of the under-determinacy of such concepts in relation to reproductive choice arises out of the fact that their meanings are sustained by and transformed within complex and relatively fluid social spaces. This means that, even were it to be possible, the interpretation of the duty to have the best possible child would be enacted within intersubjective and socially embedded discourses about human flourishing and about what it would mean for a life to go well, and there is good reason to think that in any even moderately diverse community no single, agreed concept of the 'best possible life' is going to be possible. This leads into the second reason why it is not possible to rank embryos in terms of their relationships with the best possible life. This is because, even were it possible, which I have argued it is not, to identify a number of key elements that might be said to be features of the best life, the diversity of

---

[35] Crisp, 1985.
[36] Kleinman, 1988: 142–4.

preferences for, and beliefs about, the relative importance of what would inevitably be an extensive range of such elements, combined with the variety of their possible interactions, means that it is not, even in theory, going to be possible to identify the rational choice with respect to any particular feature of an embryo or a possible child.[37]

What these two arguments mean, taken together, is that it is not possible to specify in any particular instance what would be involved in making a reproductive choice that respected the principle of procreative beneficence as conceptualized by Savulescu. This is not of course to suggest that nothing can meaningfully be said on the basis of experience about the conditions under which a good life would be more or less likely or even to suggest that there could be no coherent concept of procreative beneficence.[38] But it is to gesture towards a very different kind of principle of procreative beneficence, one which, drawing on Mill, suggests that rather than having a duty to have the child with the best opportunity of the best possible life, those who are contemplating pregnancy might be said to have no more than an obligation to consider carefully on the basis of experience, that is on the basis of their own and others' 'experiments of living', whether it is reasonable to expect that the child they are thinking of conceiving is going to have an ordinary chance of a desirable existence.[39] This also usefully reminds us that the conditions conducive to the possibility of a good life are at least as much to do with the broader social, political, economic, and environmental contexts in which people live as they are to do with their biological make-up. I shall return to this point later.

---

[37] Sen, 1999b.
[38] Nussbaum, 2000.
[39] Glover, 2006; Parker, 2007.

(ii) The concept of the 'best possible child' is paradoxical

In *All's Well that Ends Well*, Shakespeare has a minor character speak the following lines, 'The web of our life is of mingled yarn, good and ill together; our virtues would be proud if our faults whipp'd them not, and our crimes would despair if they were not cherish'd by our virtues.'[40] In this Shakespeare is not simply reminding us that human lives are by their very nature characterized by both good and ill, and that we must learn to live with these aspects of ourselves and of those around us. He makes the stronger and ultimately more interesting claim that both strengths and weaknesses of character, and of our lives more broadly, are essential and interdependent elements of the good life. Both aspects of our lives are interwoven and indeed it is this interweaving and our struggles with it that make us what we are and constitutes in its interplay of light and dark much that is of value and significance in human existence. In these lines, as in so many others, Shakespeare captures something profound and complex about human existence and in particular about our relationships with ourselves. For he suggests that it is only through recognition of the fact that we are in our nature and in our particularity both light and dark, that we come to feel both an appropriate humility and a sense of genuine self-worth. It is here too that we forge our identity.

What Shakespeare helps us to see is that in addition to being underdetermining, the concept of the best possible life is deeply paradoxical. The best possible life is not necessarily and indeed could not be one in which all goes well. The best possible life is not necessarily, indeed, could not be, one lived by a person with no flaws of character, or of biology. This is not to say that the best possible life would be one in which a certain number of character flaws were 'thrown into the mix', for example through genetic engineering or 'therapy', but rather to highlight, on the basis of

40 W. Shakespeare, *All's Well that Ends Well*, 4. 3. 68–71.

experience, the complex, organic, and profoundly paradoxical nature of the good life and of human flourishing.

The lesson to be learned from Shakespeare here is one that complements in significant ways the conclusion of the arguments above, that is, that there is no simple correlation between the features of an embryo and a good life. For it again suggests that while it may be possible to specify some conditions without which a life, any life, would be unlikely to go well, and while it may be possible in retrospect to say of a life that it was a good one, lived well, the good life is going inevitably in all cases, whatever else might be true about it, to be a 'mingled yarn' of good and ill together.

(iii) The pursuit of the 'best possible life' is self-defeating

Savulescu's commitment to the principle of procreative beneficence needs to be understood against the background of his programmatic commitment to welfare maximization and enhancement.[41] The arguments above have raised significant doubts about the possibility of specifying in advance, or even as a life progresses, in any objective way, whether it constitutes the best possible life. First, there will in most cases be legitimate disagreement and uncertainty about what constitutes the good or the best and, secondly, any coherent account of the good life will inevitably be complex. These two arguments hint also at a third. They suggest that the active pursuit of the best possible life will be likely in practice to be disorienting. For, if we take seriously Shakespeare's evocation of the breadth, depth, and paradoxical complexity of what it means to live a good life and also the inevitability of genuine uncertainty, the pursuit of the 'best possible' will always be in important respects quixotic and unlikely therefore in practice to be conducive to the good. Again, we know

---

[41] Savulescu, 2005.

from experience, from experiments of living, that the relentless pursuit of the best possible can be the enemy of the good.

A different way of capturing this insight, in consequentialist terms, would be to point out that any consideration of the good life would need to factor in the effects of perfectionism itself and it seems very likely that the active pursuit of the 'best possible' in each and every aspect of one's life, including the selection of the characteristics of one's offspring, would not only make it less likely that the 'best possible' would be achieved, but might also make even the achievement of the 'good enough' difficult. For, as none of us can be sure that we are living the best of all possible lives, the pursuit of the best possible, as opposed to the pursuit of the good, would be bound to lead to a life of dissatisfaction with any life as lived and to a constant drive for self-improvement which would inevitably be both exhausting and unlikely to lead to stable, satisfying, or deep interpersonal relationships with one's children or one's self. From a consequentialist point of view it is not impossible that there might be a tension between the pursuit of the best possible and the achievement of the good.

The argument that there is a duty to select the child with the best opportunity of the best life should be rejected. Savulescu's account of procreative beneficence is underdetermining, paradoxical, and self-defeating. It also fails to take experience sufficiently seriously. This should not however be taken to imply that beneficence is not an important moral dimension of reproductive choice. For while there is every good reason to reject the pursuit of the best possible life, this is very far from arguing that nothing at all can be usefully said on the basis of experience about the factors which contribute to the conditions under which it is possible for a life to go well. And, if it is possible to say something meaningful about the kinds of things that tend to make lives go badly or well, beneficence will have a role to play in reproductive ethics and potential parents will have an obligation to ensure, insofar as this is possible, that any child they have has at least an ordinary chance of a desirable existence.

Our understanding of what it means for a life to go well is related to our understanding and use of concepts such those of the 'good life' and of 'human flourishing'. These are complex and interdependent concepts whose meanings are sustained and transformed within social and cultural practices and this implies that the interpretation of the implications of beneficence, that is, the assessment of whether any particular possible child has an ordinary chance of a desirable existence will be inseparable from such practices and will inevitably be highly contextual. Just as conceptions of the good vary to some degree between individuals, families, communities, etc., so too will legitimate beliefs about what it means to secure the conditions for the good in particular cases, and this implies that procreative beneficence will generate somewhat different obligations in different contexts. Nevertheless, this diversity notwithstanding, the practices of communities, societies, and individuals must, if procreative beneficence is to do any work, be criticizable on the grounds of beneficence in at least some cases, that is, to the degree to which the conditions into which a child would be born can be said objectively not to be conducive to the possibility of a desirable existence.[42] What this means is that a coherent account of procreative beneficence is, in addition to recognizing the social and contextual aspects of procreative beneficence, going to be one that allows space for consideration of the objective conditions required for the possibility of the flourishing of *any* human life.[43]

Conclusion

In response to the case of Sharon Duchesneau and Candy McCullough, Julian Savulescu argues for two principles of reproductive ethics: reproductive autonomy and procreative beneficence where the principle of procreative beneficence is conceptualized in terms

---

[42] Sen, 1999a.
[43] Nussbaum, 2000.

of a duty to *have the child, of the possible children we could have, who will have the best opportunity of the best life*. Savulescu goes on to argue that while Sharon should be free to make the choice she did, that is, to have a deaf child, and the woman who is a carrier of SED should be free to choose to implant any of her embryos, that is, to choose to have a child of short stature, both women in fact have a duty, grounded in respect for procreative beneficence, to choose the child with the best opportunity of the best life, that is, the non-disabled child. In this chapter, I have argued that this duty should be rejected. Beneficence does nonetheless have an important role to play in reproductive ethics. For, insofar as we have reason to believe on the basis of experience and previous 'experiments of living' that it is possible to say something meaningful about the conditions for a desirable existence, beneficence requires of us that, where we have a choice, we ensure that our children grow up under such conditions.

While reproductive libertarians such as Savulescu draw heavily upon Mill's concept of 'experiments of living' to justify their emphasis on the importance of respect for reproductive autonomy, they strikingly fail to take such experiments and the things they tell us about what makes a life go badly or well sufficiently seriously. Mill argued that experiments of living were key to understanding the requirements of reproductive beneficence. For reproductive libertarians, because all experiments of living lie in the unexplored and unreachable future, there is little to be learned from them. The call for experiments in living only makes sense if their purpose is to do real moral work in the present, that is, if we are willing to take the lessons of such experiments, and of experience, seriously. If we do this, the duty to choose the best possible child becomes a less seductive interpretation of the principle of reproductive beneficence.

In some cases, such as the two described at the beginning of this chapter, third parties will be involved in the process of bringing about a life. In the case of Sharon and Candy this was a friend who provided the sperm; in the case of the woman who is a carrier of

SED it was the IVF clinic, which had the technology to carry out PGD. In such cases, the social location of the choice introduces another moral dimension and the third parties involved come to have relevant moral obligations. In most cases these will simply require, where resources permit and where there is a reasonable chance that any resulting child will have a desirable existence, helping these women to have a child they could not otherwise have.

But, where health professionals have concerns about this, it will be incumbent upon them to help potential parents to think carefully about the life they are about to create. The health professionals involved will have obligations to encourage people to reflect on their choices, to give reasons, and to debate with them the moral dimensions of their choices. While it might be argued by some that this is an infringement of patient autonomy, that is, of reproductive liberty, this is not the case. It is more respectful of autonomy to discuss the reasons people have for making a choice and to challenge choices that seem unreflective than it is to simply accept such choices at face value. Such challenging can be conducive to the patient's developing understanding and respectful of their ability to change their mind in the light of good reasoning.

In some very rare cases it will be right for the health service to refuse to provide a service, whatever justification potential parents give. That is, there are situations in which even against a broad background commitment to reproductive autonomy beneficence trumps liberty. Examples will include cases in which potential parents choose to have children whose lives can be foreseen to be intolerable. It would, for example, to take an extreme case, be morally required of a health service to refuse to provide treatment that would enable a woman to choose deliberately to have a child with Edwards' syndrome, or Trisomy 13, given the current unavailability of effective interventions. In most cases of reproductive decision-making however, that is, those in which it might reasonably be argued that the conditions for the possibility of a desirable existence have been met, these are choices that women should be free to make on the basis of their own values and experience, and in the light of their own conceptions of what it means for a life to go well. In Sharon and Candy's case, this appears to be what they attempted in good faith to do. The case of deafness, even within the context of a supportive deaf community, is nevertheless a very difficult and possibly limiting case, one which inevitably raises the question of whether the resulting child does indeed have an ordinary chance of a desirable existence.

The focus of this chapter has been on the obligations that people thinking of becoming parents through the use of assisted reproductive technologies might reasonably be said to have with respect to the lives of the children they are considering bringing into existence. I have argued against Savulescu's assertion that parents have an obligation to have the child, of the possible children they could have, who will have the best opportunity of the best life, in favour of a principle of reproductive beneficence such that parents have an obligation to ensure, insofar as this is possible, that any child they have has at least the ordinary chance of a desirable existence. Whilst this is in a sense a less demanding formulation of the principle of reproductive beneficence than that proposed by Savulescu, it does nevertheless place substantive moral demands upon potential parents, reflecting the real moral significance of the decision to have a child.

Whilst the formulation of the principle of reproductive beneficence outlined above offers a more coherent way of thinking about moral decision-making in the context of assisted reproduction, this chapter has inevitably left a number of important issues unexplored and a number of important questions unanswered. It has, in particular, not addressed the implications of the principle of reproductive beneficence outlined above for reproductive decision-making outside of the context of assisted reproductive technologies. What, for example, are the implications of this formulation of the principle for potential parents who live in situations, such as those of desperate poverty, which, whilst beyond their control, mean that any child of theirs is likely to live a life of tremendous hardship? How is the principle to be interpreted in such circumstances? What, for example, is to be understood by the 'ordinary chance of a desirable existence' as relative to the particular circumstances in which a child is to be raised? How are the reproductive obligations of women in such circumstances affected by the realities of the social, economic, and cultural constraints on their reproductive autonomy? Furthermore, what, given the socio-political features of such contexts, are the extent and nature of the obligations that agents other than the potential parents owe both to potential parents and their future children? Whilst these questions are beyond the scope of the current chapter they are ones to which I intend to return in future papers.

4

The Limits of Reproductive Freedom

DAVID BENATAR

Introduction

It is only relatively recently, and then only in some jurisdictions, that a right to reproductive freedom has been recognized. This hard-won freedom was preceded by a long history of unwarranted interference in reproduction, often justified by pseudo-science and arising from notorious bias. A right to reproductive freedom is a welcome corrective to this.

However, where a right to reproductive freedom has been acknowledged and entrenched, reproductive freedom has been accorded too much value and given excessive protection. Whereas it is widely recognized that other (similarly hard-won) freedoms must be bounded by the interests of those who would be wronged by the unrestricted use of those freedoms, reproductive freedom is not, but should be, subject to similar constraints.

Thus it is unheard of (in places where a right to reproductive freedom is acknowledged) to interfere with reproductive freedom, even where this freedom results in suffering offspring. Moreover, many philosophers and the courts have tended to reject wrongful life claims. These are claims brought against parents or doctors for having allowed somebody to come into existence when it should have been known that the life started would be one of great hardship.[1] Although it is readily acknowledged that inflicting a severe hardship on an already existent person would clearly be wrong and would merit legal action, inflicting that same hardship on a future person by bringing that person into existence is treated quite differently.

Indeed, many people are reluctant even to criticize harmful reproductive conduct. If a woman subjected her existent child to a significant chance of contracting a life-threatening disease she would be roundly condemned and charged with child endangerment (at the very least). Yet if a woman conceives a child that has the same chance of suffering from a life-threatening condition such as AIDS, it is thought inappropriate by many people even to criticize her action.[2] Some go so far as to say that HIV-positive women have a right to *assisted*-reproduction.[3]

I shall argue that it is unacceptable to attach such vastly discrepant weight to the interests of present and future people. Thus, if it is wrong to inflict a particular hardship on an existent person then, barring any special considerations, it is wrong to inflict the same hardship on a future person. In arguing for this conclusion I shall raise and respond to two influential arguments for opposing views.

The first of these opposing arguments denies that one can harm people by bringing them into existence. It is said to follow that the interests of future people need not—indeed, cannot—be considered when deciding whether to perform an action that will bring into existence a suffering person. The second argument to which I shall respond allows for the interests of future people to be

---

[1] Although the child already exists when the action is brought, what is evaluated is the earlier action that allegedly failed to consider the interests of that child while it was still a future (possible) child.

[2] Levine and Dubler, 1990; Allen, 1996.

[3] See e.g. Myer and Moroni, 2005; Nosarka et al., 2007. These authors do suggest that assisting HIV-positive people in reproducing should be coupled with efforts to reduce the risk of transmission. They also consider the potential harm to the child of being born to parents with a shortened life expectancy. However, they argue that current treatment options can significantly extend life expectancy, rendering HIV a chronic rather than a fatal disease. What they do not consider is the possibility of emergent resistance to current anti-retrovirals and the impact that would have on the life-span of HIV-positive people.

considered, but denies that those interests can defeat the right to reproductive freedom enjoyed by those who would bring these people into existence.

In arguing that the interests of future people, all things being equal, should count the same as the interests of present people, I am not committed to opposing abortion. This is because my argument does not commit me to any particular view about foetal moral status. If, as I happen to think, early foetuses lack moral standing—if, that is, they have not yet come into existence in the morally relevant sense—then one can accept the equality of present and future people's interests while permitting abortion. That is to say, one can claim that, all things being equal, future people should not be harmed, and yet deny that preventing future people from coming into existence harms them. In other words, one can think that a person is at liberty to prevent a future possible person from becoming actual—by not conceiving it or by aborting it—while denying that people may do things that will harm people who will come into existence.

Non-Identity

The first argument against my position could be construed, in principle, as allowing the interests of present and future people to be treated equally. However, it suggests that special considerations apply to actions that *bring about* future people,[4] the upshot of which is that people cannot be harmed by being brought into existence even if they will suffer considerable hardships. The argument, which draws on the now famous 'non-identity' problem,[5] takes the following form.

---

[4] By contrast, the argument does not apply to actions that inflict hardship on a future person who will exist whether or not that action is performed.

[5] Although the term 'non-identity problem' is Derek Parfit's (1984: ch. 16), the problem itself has been widely recognized and has long plagued so-called 'wrongful life' suits.

1. For something to harm somebody, it must make that person worse off.
2. The 'worse off' relation is a relation between two states.
3. Thus, for somebody to be worse off in some state (such as existence), the alternative state, with which it is compared, must be one in which he is less badly (or better) off.
4. But non-existence is not a state in which anybody can be, and thus cannot be compared with existence.
5. Thus coming into existence cannot be *worse* than never coming into existence.
6. Therefore, coming into existence cannot be a harm.

Those who advance this argument acknowledge that bringing suffering people into existence may increase the amount of pain and distress in the world, and thus produce worse consequences than not bringing them into existence. Although such a state of affairs is worse, no *person* is worse off or harmed. The non-identity argument thus poses a challenge to those, namely liberals, who think that freedom may be restricted only in order to prevent wrongful harm,[6] rather than to make the world better (or less bad). It also poses a problem for wrongful life torts. Because there is alleged to be nobody who can claim to have been harmed, there is nobody with standing to sue.

There are a variety of ways of responding to this problem and thus it is unclear that it should stand in the way of restricting a right to reproductive freedom where the unlimited right causes suffering people. One approach to the problem is to tackle it head on. Although many have feared that the non-identity argument is unassailable, there are at least two separate ways of criticizing it and thus of solving the non-identity problem.

---

[6] This is an oversimplification. Most liberals accept not only a 'harm principle', outlined here, but also some, highly restricted 'offence principle'. According to the latter, *some* offensive conduct may also be regulated, even though not outright prohibited. My oversimplification is not problematic in the current context, because the problem at hand could not be solved by the addition of a (qualified) offence principle.

The first of these is to deny that the conception of harm asserted in the argument's first premise is the only possible one. Although this account of harm works well in most cases it clearly cannot account for procreative harm. If no alternative account of harm were possible then we would have to accept that procreative harm were impossible. However, an alternative *is* possible. On this alternative account, harm can be inflicted in one of two ways. The first and most common way is specified in the first premise of the non-identity argument. The second way somebody can be harmed is: (i) by a condition that is bad for him; where (ii) the alternative would not have been bad.[7] According to this view of harm, it makes no difference that the alternative to somebody's having existed with the hardship is that this person would not have come into existence at all. This is because the hardship is bad for him and the alternative (non-existence) would not have been bad. It does not matter that the reason why the alternative (non-existence) would not have been bad is that he would not have existed. This is because it is not necessary that the alternative to somebody's being in a bad state is that he *is* (that is, that he exists) in a state that is not bad (or is less bad). Instead it is sufficient that the alternative to his being in a bad state is that there is a possible state of affairs (whether or not he is in it) that is not bad for him. A state in which somebody never existed cannot possibly be bad for him.

The second way to respond to the non-identity argument is to reject the second (and thus also the third) premise. One could deny that to be worse off in some condition one must have existed in the alternative condition with which it is compared. On this view what is meant by the claim that somebody is worse off having come into existence is that never existing would have been *preferable*. In defending this view, Joel Feinberg offers an analogy with *ceasing* to exist.[8] When it is said that somebody would be better off dead,

---

[7] Derek Parfit makes a similar move, but with reference to 'better' rather than 'worse' (1984: 489).

[8] Feinberg, 1992.

one does not mean that that person would exist in some better condition were he to die. Instead one means that the condition of not existing would be preferable to continued existence. Just as it might be better for somebody that he cease to exist, so it might be better for somebody that he never come into existence. That is to say, when one compares the scenario in which the person comes into existence with the alternative scenario in which he never exists and one evaluates these scenarios in terms of the interests of the person who exists only in the first scenario, one judges the second scenario to be preferable.[9]

If these responses to the non–identity argument are successful, then it is possible to harm somebody by bringing him into existence if his life will be of a poor quality. I have not said anything about how bad a condition needs to be in order for a life inseparable from such a condition to be harmful. There is room for disagreement about this.[10] Rather than attempting to resolve that disagreement, I have sought only to show that the non–identity problem is resolvable.

Those who are unconvinced that the non–identity problem can be solved may still justify restrictions on the right to reproductive freedom where this is necessary to prevent (or compensate) suffering people. Joel Feinberg has argued that liberals who deny that one can be harmed by being brought into existence might decide to allow 'a clear categorical exception' to the liberal requirement that actions be legally prohibited only when they (wrongfully) harm people.[11] He says that liberalism 'might still apply exceptionlessly to the postnatal world, but for actions and omissions that lead to the existence of new human beings' an exception may reasonably be made. He recognizes that this is 'an untidy solution' but denies

---

[9] I discuss these matters in much greater detail in Benatar, 2006.

[10] I have argued elsewhere (ibid.) that coming into existence is *always* a harm. I do not presuppose that view here. Indeed, my aim is to show that, even if one denies my views that coming into existence is always a harm and that it is always wrong to have children, one should still think that reproductive freedom should be limited.

[11] Feinberg, 1990: 327.

that it is *suspiciously ad hoc*. This, he says, is because there is 'something very special about 'harmful conception' that might lead us to
expect that its peculiarities will not be repeated elsewhere. It is the
only example we can have of a person's being put in a harmful
condition by the very act that brings him into existence, and the
only example where determinations of harm require comparison of
a given condition with no existence at all.'[12]

There is much to be said for making such an exception (if one
believes that one cannot be harmed by being brought into existence). The non-identity problem clearly is a *problem*. Those who
think that non-identity implies that people can never be harmed by
being brought into existence are not (and should not be) comfort-
able with this conclusion, at least where the quality of life is bad
enough. They (should) recognize that, like paradoxes, it presents a
problem in need of a solution. If the problem cannot be solved, we
are faced with the choice of either allowing people to cause vast
amounts of suffering because technically nobody is harmed, or we
do not allow a technicality to stand in the way of preventing this
suffering.

In summary, then, it seems that the non-identity problem can be
solved. However, those who are unconvinced may still have reason
to prohibit bringing into existence people whose lives will be lives
of suffering.

Reproductive Rights

A more popular challenge to my view comes from the prevailing
view about the scope and strength of reproductive rights. Although
defenders of an expansive and robust right to reproductive freedom
can advance the non-identity argument, they need not do so. They
can allow that the interests of future people are morally considerable and that future people may indeed be harmed by the

---

[12] Feinberg, 1990: 327.

reproductive decisions of those who bring them into existence. Yet they may deny that the interests of those future people are sufficiently strong to restrict or override the right of the reproducers to reproductive freedom. In other words, some defenders of reproductive rights might object that the evidence I proffered for my claim that future people's interests are underweighted is not in fact evidence for that claim. Instead, they might say, it is evidence of how much importance they attach to reproductive rights.

Although I agree that reproductive rights are important, I shall argue that the actual extent of their importance is insufficient to outweigh the interests of future people in all the circumstances that they are thought to do just this. The implication is that the interests of future people are being accorded too little weight, either intrinsically or relative to reproductive rights. Reproductive freedom has been given excessive scope and strength and has been ascribed too widely.

Consider, first, the scope of a right to reproductive freedom. A right to such freedom can be understood more narrowly or more broadly. Under the narrowest construal, the right includes only the first one or two of the rights below. Under the broadest construal, it includes all of them.

1. A right against direct physical interferences with one's reproductive choices

A right against direct physical interferences precludes physically forced impregnation (artificially or otherwise), the forced implantation of a contraceptive device, involuntary surgical sterilization, involuntary abortion, and physical restraint to prevent abortion.

2. A right against indirect physical interferences with one's reproductive choices

Direct physical force is not the only way to impose burdens of the kind prohibited by the right against direct physical interferences. Legal and other measures, where they are backed up by physical force, employ physical force indirectly to secure the same ends. For example, the criminal law might prohibit abortion, thereby forcing a woman to endure a pregnancy she does not wish to continue. Although it may sometimes be *possible* for somebody to act contrary to these interferences, she may then face a physical interference (such as imprisonment) that is at least as bad, if not worse, than that which the law would have her endure.

3. A right against unobtrusive interferences with one's reproductive choices

Not all interferences with reproductive choices need be as obtrusive as the right against direct physical interference always is and as the right against indirect physical interference usually is. Adding contraceptives or abortifacients to the drinking water system or the food supply are examples of unobtrusive practices that could interfere with reproductive choices.[13] A right against unobtrusive interferences would protect against such practices.

4. A right against moderate coercion regarding one's reproductive choices

As I have described it, a right against indirect physical interferences is a right against extreme coercion. Given that coercion manifests along a spectrum from the most extreme to the most mild, there are indefinitely many degrees of coercion. For simplicity's sake, I speak here only of moderate coercion in order to distinguish it from the most extreme form. Moderate coercion is distinguishable from extreme coercion primarily by the (greater) degree to which it may still be feasible to choose the option one is being coerced to avoid.

5. A right against moral criticism of one's reproductive choices

It is sometimes thought that criticism of one's reproductive choices (at least prospectively) constitutes a kind of interference with those

---

[13] These two practices are both physical interferences. However, mental interferences are also possible. Consider e.g. hypnotic suggestion (either to abstain from or to undertake reproduction).

choices. That claim is sometimes plausible, although in many instances only those who are the most impressionable or who have the thinnest skin can be 'coerced' by moral criticism. However the question whether moral criticism constitutes an interference is distinct from the question whether that interference is warranted. If it is not, then one might be said to have a right against having one's reproductive choices criticized. Here it is important to distinguish between a moral right and a legal right to reproductive freedom. If somebody has a moral right to reproduce then exercise of that right is beyond even moral reproach. However, if a person has (or ought to have) a legal right to reproductive freedom then, although exercise of that right is beyond legal reproach, it is not necessarily beyond moral reproach.

6. A right against directive counselling regarding one's reproductive choices

It is rarely thought that merely presenting reproductive options to people constitutes an interference with their freedom. However, it is sometimes thought that *recommending* one option over another does constitute such an interference.[14] This is the view that has characterized genetic counselling, which has attempted to be steadfastly neutral and non-directive. Those who think that directive counselling constitutes not only an interference but also an unwarranted one will suggest that there is a right against such directive counselling.

7. A right to assistance in reproducing

In contrast to the first six interpretations of a right to reproductive freedom, which understand the right as a negative one, the seventh interpretation understands the right as a positive one. On this view,

---

[14] e.g. Kathleen Nolan says that 'the imposition of unwanted advice by a paternalistic counsellor may...violate the ethical principles of autonomy and procreative freedom' (1989: 63). Nancy Kass says that 'it is not appropriate to voice a professional opinion as part of the information automatically provided' (1991: 323). London et al., 2008: 17, say that 'counselling that is directive and discourages HIV-positive women and men from making free choices about whether to have a child violates their rights to reproductive autonomy'.

one has a positive entitlement to aid in one's decision to reproduce. (I do not have in mind here ante- and peri-natal healthcare aimed at fostering maternal health, but rather assisted reproduction.)

To clarify, I am not suggesting that this is an exhaustive list—nor that it is the only possible taxonomy of the differing views of the scope of a right to reproductive freedom. However, I hope that it does capture the most important categories. They are arranged in (roughly) descending order of importance. That is to say, the earlier interpretations protect against the worse interferences whereas the later interpretations protect against the lesser interferences or secure some positive (but arguably lesser) good. I say that it is *roughly* descending order, because there may be some dispute about some of the ordering. (For instance, the burdens of violating (2) would sometimes be as great as the burdens of violating (1). Similarly, depending on how sensitive a given person is to criticism and how much he or she wants a baby, (7) might be thought to be more important than (5) or (6).) However, to the extent that there could be agreement on the ordering, the least controversial interpretation of the right to reproductive freedom would be the one at the top of the list. More expansive interpretations of the scope of this right would include not only that interpretation but also additional subsequent ones.

So far I have focused on the *scope of a right* to reproductive freedom. A second important consideration is the strength of any such right—that is, how important a consideration it is relative to other moral considerations. The stronger a right the greater moral capacity it has to trump other considerations. The scope and the strength of the right are linked in the following way: All things being equal, the broader the scope of the right, the weaker the outer limits of the right will be. A right to assistance in reproducing will be more readily defeated than a right against direct physical interference with one's reproductive choices.

The third important consideration pertains to the *bearer of the right*. Questions about the scope and strength of a right to reproductive freedom are questions about the right itself. However there are also questions about who bears a right of a particular scope and strength. Children are not thought, according to the dominant view, to have a right to reproductive freedom, although the adults they will become are thought to have such a right. As a result, children may now have no right to reproductive freedom, although they may have a right to an open reproductive future (to adapt Joel Feinberg's phrase). Nevertheless, there are questions about other categories of people. For example, do the profoundly retarded have a right to reproduce? Or would involuntary sterilization in such cases be permissible—or even morally required?

I shall argue that if we take seriously the interests of future people, then common views about the scope, strength, and bearers of the right to reproductive freedom should be reconsidered. For instance, the reticence of many people to suggest that it is *ever* wrong for an adult or late adolescent to reproduce is overly indulgent. The claim that people are entitled to positive assistance in reproducing even if they stand a high chance of producing diseased or impaired offspring gives excessive weight to procreative interests and much too little weight to the interests of those who are brought into existence.

Is there any way of reconciling an extensive and strong right to reproductive freedom with a commitment to appropriate consideration of the interests of future people? There are a number of arguments that might be advanced to suggest that reproduction is indeed different and thus should be treated differently from instances of non-reproductive harm. As a result, it might be said, the interests of future people, although important, cannot defeat a right to reproductive freedom. I shall raise and respond to four such arguments.

Autonomy

A right to reproductive freedom is often justified with reference to a principle of autonomy. In other words, it is argued that given the importance of autonomy—deciding for oneself and acting in accordance with one's decisions—it is not the place of other citizens or the state to dictate to a competent adult that he or she may not produce children. Although the interests of future people are important, we simply may not violate people's autonomy.

Autonomy is indeed an important principle and should be protected from arbitrary violation. However, the principle of autonomy has a limited scope. Those committed to the freedom of competent adults to do as they please typically recognize that this freedom must be limited by the rights of others. One has a right to do as one pleases as long as what pleases one does not harm others unjustifiably or stand a great chance of doing so. One does not, for example, have a right to maim or kill people or to risk doing so by driving recklessly. Thus it is far from clear that a right to reproductive freedom that is grounded on a principle of autonomy or liberty can include a right to reproduce where the offspring stand a high chance of being harmed. It is curious, therefore, that at least some of those who agree that we have no right to put others at significant risk of harm in non-reproductive contexts nonetheless think that we may put others at the same risk of harm in reproductive contexts. They employ a double standard in these two contexts.

Some might wish to distinguish between reproductive contexts and other contexts by arguing that reproductive interests are particularly important interests (and thus may override other interests more easily).[15] However, this argument is doomed to failure. At least some other interests, including interests in political or religious freedom, that conflict with other people's interests are surely at least as important to some people as are interests in reproductive freedom. Yet religious and political freedom may not be invoked to defend practices that stand a great chance of inflicting considerable harm on others.[16]

---

[15] Among those who take this view are those who argue that a right to reproductive freedom is based not on autonomy but rather directly on reproductive interests, which are taken to be of special importance. See Robertson, 1994: esp. 24–5.

[16] My claim is not that people *do* not invoke religious and political freedom to justify practices that inflict significant harm on others. My claim is that they *may* not do so.

Curiously, those who frown on criticism of reproductive conduct sometimes do so precisely because they allege that that conduct is *not* autonomous. Responding to a suggestion[17] that a homeless, possibly HIV-positive, crack addict whose three previous children are in foster care and who gives birth to another child is 'a paradigmatic case of parental irresponsibility' and that the woman 'has no business having children',[18] one commentator[19] has suggested that this woman is not blameworthy precisely because she is not an autonomous moral decision-maker. Her choice to have another child is really a 'non-choice'.[20]

In assessing this argument it is helpful to distinguish between whether an action is wrong and whether it is blameworthy. An action is wrong if it is an action that should not have been performed. However, sometimes a person cannot be blamed for performing a wrongful action. One possible explanation is that the person lacked the competence to be culpable for the action. If, for example, a toddler finds a firearm in the house and fires the weapon killing the parent who left it lying around, then we might say that although the firing of the gun was the wrong action—in the sense that it was an action that should not have been performed—we certainly cannot say that the child should be blamed for performing it. The child simply did not know what he or she was doing.

Perhaps the suggestion, then, is that if the crack-addicted woman, on account of her drug dependence and her dire social circumstances, is unable to make a reasoned decision about whether to become pregnant and whether to terminate the pregnancy, she cannot be blamed for having the child. Notice, however, that if her

---

Typically, those defending a religious practice will deny that it significantly harms others. If they are correct, then religious freedom may indeed justify the practice. However, if they are incorrect, then liberals would typically deny that religious freedom could justify the practice. For more on weighing cultural and religious practices versus practices that (are said to) harm children, see Benatar and Benatar, 2003.

[17] By Arras, 1990.
[18] Ibid. 370.
[19] Allen, 1996.
[20] Ibid. 379.

child-bearing is not blameworthy because it is not autonomous, then it would not be a violation of her autonomy to prevent her from reproducing. Unless some alternative explanation can be provided why her non-autonomous actions should be protected by a right to reproductive freedom, then by showing that she is not blameworthy one has also shown that she should not enjoy a right to have children. In other words, the implication of claiming that the action is not blameworthy is that the interference with her reproductive freedom is not wrong. For those fighting for a robust right to reproductive freedom, this outcome might be a battle won but a war lost.[21]

We might ask, however, whether the crack-addict's child-bearing is indeed non-autonomous. Is she really in the category of the toddler who has no idea about what a gun is, about what pulling the trigger will do, and so forth? Whether the crack-addict is autonomous depends on one's conception of 'autonomy'. If one understands it maximally to refer to highly sophisticated reasoning on the basis of highly reliable information in the absence of any influences external to the pure will of the moral agent, then the woman is clearly not autonomous. However, that conception of autonomy is clearly too demanding, for very few if any decisions by anybody would be autonomous by that standard. Nor is the woman as incompetent and ignorant as the toddler. Thus the question is whether she has sufficient understanding and control, such that her conduct can be designated as autonomous. If it can, then her conduct is blameworthy. Otherwise, because her action is not blameworthy it may be permissible for others to prevent it. If one prefers to understand 'autonomy' as a scale rather than a threshold concept, then her action might be blameworthy to some extent,

---

[21] Those who ground a right to reproductive freedom directly in reproductive interests, rather than in autonomy, fare only marginally better. Although restricting the reproductive freedom of those who would reproduce non-autonomously would still thwart their reproductive interests, it is not clear, for reasons mentioned earlier, why these interests ought to prevail over the interests of those who will be harmed if the right to reproductive freedom is not limited.

but no further. However, the extent to which it is not blameworthy is also the extent to which interferences may be warranted.

Causal connections

A second argument why instances of reproductive harm should be treated differently from instances of non-reproductive harm is epistemological. It makes the claim that although reproductive harm is possible it is harder to demonstrate when such harm has been caused. Thus, although in principle we should treat reproductive harm the same as other harm, in practice this is not possible. How, for example, does one know whether a premature birth and the child's low birth-weight should be attributable to maternal irresponsibility or to back luck?

In response to this argument it can be noted that, although there are some instances where we cannot be sure of the causal connection between somebody's action and the harm to the resultant child, there are other instances of reproductive harm where this is not the case. The causal damage trans-placentally is often easier to prove than in other contexts. For instance, it is quite clear, when a child is born with foetal alcohol syndrome, what caused it. Similarly, an HIV-positive infant, barring a transfusion, sexual assault, or some other exceptional circumstance, is the victim of mother-to-child transmission. Other procreative harm is not inflicted via conception, gestation, and parturition. Consider, for example, a child born into dire poverty, such that his or her parents are unable to provide adequate nutrition and shelter. Such a child is harmed by the procreative activities of its parents (unless one of the parties did not consent either to those activities or to the birth of the child).

Moral costs

A third argument for treating reproductive harm differently from harm in other contexts also acknowledges the tragedy of reproductive harm. However, according to this argument the moral costs of intervening to prevent or punish such harmful conduct are so great that such interventions would be still more tragic than the harm they seek to prevent. According to this argument, the same cannot be said of interventions to prevent other kinds of harm.

This argument is extremely compelling when it is used to defend a right to reproductive freedom in its *narrower* senses. The moral costs of forced sterilization, forced abortion, and the invasions of privacy that would be required to determine whether alcohol-consuming or tobacco-smoking women are pregnant (and thus engaging in harmful behaviour) are immense. If any of these measures were to be adopted in a bid to prevent or punish harmful reproductive conduct, the moral costs could very plausibly be thought to outweigh the harms they were undertaken to prevent.

However, the argument becomes less compelling as the scope of the right is increased to protect against interventions of diminishing severity. Unobtrusive interventions and moderate coercion are far from obviously worse than the harms they might prevent. It is highly implausible that the costs of directive counselling or moral criticism of one's actions are so great that they outweigh profound harms to future persons. And it seems outrageous to say that such harms are outweighed by the costs of withholding assistance in reproduction.

Lest anybody wonder how moderate coercion, directive counselling, or moral criticism could possibly be thought justifiable, consider, by analogy, a conflict between a duty of medical confidentiality and a duty to prevent serious harm to a third party. It is widely recognized that medical confidentiality is not an absolute principle and that it may be breached in some select circumstances. It is also widely recognized that in such circumstances persuading a patient to give permission for the information to be disclosed is preferable to disclosing the information without the patient's (reluctant) permission. It is at least sometimes permissible to coerce moderately a patient into providing such consent. It is more often permissible to recommend that they do and to criticize their refusal to do so. There are obvious moral costs in taking such steps, but if conveying the information is sufficiently important—if it prevents a harm of sufficient magnitude—then the moral costs are deemed acceptable. If that is the case in the context of non-reproductive harm, why should it not also be the case in reproductive harm?

Now there may be disagreement about how much harm or what risk of harm is sufficiently serious to warrant interference with reproductive freedom. However, there is similar disagreement about how to weigh up harms against other freedoms. In other words, the fact of disagreement is not unique to reproductive freedom and thus cannot be cited as a basis for treating a right to reproductive freedom differently.

Moral difference

A fourth argument seeks to show that we may not find fault with the reproductive decisions of others because their values may be different from our own. The implicit assumption is that an action that may be wrong for oneself may not be wrong for those who hold different views.[22]

The claim that 'X *is wrong for* Y (but *not wrong for* Z)' is notoriously ambiguous. It may mean either:

(a) Y regards X as wrong (but Z does not regard X as wrong); or
(b) it is actually wrong for Y (but not for Z) to perform X.

If it is (a) that is meant, then all we are being told is that there are some people who do not (appear to) to think that it is wrong to bring damaged children into existence. This might explain why they bring children into existence despite the risk of serious harm. However, an *explanation* why people act in the way they do is not a *justification* of those actions. In other words simply telling us that there are people who think it is acceptable to produce damaged

---

[22] Something like this view is defended by Levine and Dubler, 1990. Authors such as this speak e.g. about the cultural value of reproduction to HIV-positive women who reproduce (1990: 334). Anita Allen says that in 'the mind of the maternalist, which is to say in the minds of vast segments of our society, there is normally a very strong, virtually irrebuttable, moral presumption in favor of motherhood' (1996: 398).

children tells nothing about whether they are correct to think that. Those who doubt this should note that there are some people who do not think that there is anything wrong in forcibly sterilizing HIV-positive women. Noting that there are people with such views says nothing about whether such views are correct.

Thus the interesting claim is not whether people have differing moral judgements, but rather whether different things are actually right and wrong for different people on account of their differing values.

An implausible interpretation of the argument for (b) is that it is an argument from moral relativism. On this view, the fact that somebody (or some culture) takes something to be right actually makes it right for him or her. This is implausible because it accords each person or each culture a moral infallibility—no culture, for example, can make a mistake in determining what is morally right for itself. Those defending this view need to explain why a culture can be mistaken about other matters but not about morality. They also need to accept that moral relativism is a two-edged sword. If it really is not wrong for some people knowingly or negligently to produce damaged offspring (because they do not think that it is wrong to do so) then it is also not wrong for those who would prevent such reproduction to do so if they think that there is nothing wrong with preventing such reproduction.

More plausible arguments for (b) will give much less weight to people's personal or cultural values in determining what it is actually, rather than merely thought to be, permissible and impermissible for them to do. This is not to say that such values have no influence on what one ought to do. One's own values, just like one other distinctive features of one's circumstance, can play some role in determining what one ought to do. However, the relationship between one's moral views and what one actually ought to do will be much more complicated than moral relativism would have us believe. Given the lesser weight that one's personal or cultural values will carry on this view, it is hard to see how those views could render a profoundly harmful act morally permissible. Nor is it

is sufficient to say, as some[23] have said, that the harm is not intended. The infliction of profound harms may be prevented even if they are not intended. Where they cannot be prevented, their infliction may be condemned even if they result only from negligence rather than an evil intention.

Determining the Scope and Strength of a Right to Reproductive Freedom

It seems, then, that we should reconceive the right to reproductive freedom, in order to limit its scope and strength, and perhaps the class of its right-bearers. To fail to do this is to misconceive future people as morally unimportant or less important. I shall not now delineate the boundaries of a right to reproductive freedom, as that is too large a task to undertake here. Instead, I shall offer some general comments about how one should approach the delineation of these limits.

In determining the correct limits of a right to reproductive freedom, we need, if we are to avoid our biases, to make two kinds of comparison. First, we must compare procreative and non-procreative cases of harms and risks of harms. If a non-procreative action is wrong because it entails a 25 per cent chance of infecting a non-consenting person with an incurable lethal disease, then procreation that carries the same risk of the same severity of harm must also be wrong. Thus procreation by two people, both of whom are carriers of a recessive gene for a lethal disease would be wrong (because the chances of producing affected children would be 25 per cent). It similarly would be wrong for an HIV positive person to procreate where the risk of transmission is similarly elevated, as it often is.[24] These risks can be reduced in certain circumstances—where, for example, the mother is taking antiretrovirals. In these

---

[23] Levine and Dubler, 1990: 346.

[24] Working Group, 1995; Garcia *et al.*, 1999.

cases, which are much more common in developed than in developing countries, the adjusted risk must be compared with similar risks of similar harms in non-procreative contexts.

The second comparison we must make is between our own conduct, whether reproductive or not, and that of other people. It is easier to minimize the significance of others' interests, whether they be the procreative interests of actual people or the interests of possible people we might create through our own procreative conduct. For example, a carrier of a genetic disease might focus on *risk* of harm, noting that the risk of harm to his or her offspring is 25 per cent whereas the risk of deprivation for the child of a pauper is much higher. However, a pauper might focus on the harm itself and judge that a life of economic deprivation is less bad than a life of disease and impairment (perhaps not noticing that deprivation often leads to disease). In other words, people are inclined to make self-serving judgements. This bias must be corrected by considering what judgement one would make about comparable risks of comparable harms from the conduct of others. However, merely imagining somebody else in exactly one's own situation is unlikely to have the required corrective effect. Thus, when one considers what judgement one would make of others, their condition should be different even though the risks and harms are the same. If, for example, one is the carrier of a genetic disease then the comparable case one considers should not also be a genetic disease. Instead one should consider a case where a comparable risk of a comparable harm is produced in different way.

A minimal condition, then, for sound judgements about the limits of procreative freedom for others is that these judgements must be consistent with judgements we make in non-procreative contexts and with judgements we make about ourselves. However, because it is possible to be consistently *wrong*, consistency is only one condition that must be met. A further condition is that of 'reasonableness'. When this test is coupled with the consistency requirement, we may sometimes find that non-reproductive conduct that risks causing harm and that we previously judged to be wrong may actually not be wrong. More often, I suspect, we shall find that reproductive conduct that causes or risks harm, and that we previously thought to be acceptable, will prove to be morally wrong.

There obviously will be a grey area in which it is hard to determine whether a given risk of a specific harm is unreasonable. In such cases one has to think more carefully while recognizing that there may be room for reasonable disagreement about what constitutes reasonableness. Yet, there will be many cases where the risk of harm is, by ordinary standards, quite clearly either reasonable or unreasonable.

The more risky and harmful procreation is, the less favourable the view we should take of it and the less tolerant we need be. Where procreation is only mildly unreasonable, we might simply desist from assisting reproduction. In worse cases we might condemn it, while in the most egregious cases we might consider prohibiting or preventing it if this can successfully be achieved without the moral costs outweighing the benefits.

The extent to which we should interfere with reproductive freedom is a product not merely of the severity of the harm that will be prevented. Where reproductive harm can be avoided equally well and efficiently by more than one kind of interference with reproductive harm, it is obviously preferable to choose the lesser interference. Thus, if we could prevent reproductive harm equally well either by physically restraining somebody or by incentivizing her in ways that some judge to be coercive, the latter would be better.

Many defenders of an unlimited or at least a very expansive and robust right to reproductive freedom will be quick to note that reproductive harm could often be prevented without *any* interference with a right to reproductive freedom. In such cases, the principles I have enunciated would preclude limiting reproductive freedom. However, there may be fewer such cases than defenders of an unlimited right to reproductive freedom think. Consider, for example, those who argue that instead of providing incentives to the poor to have themselves sterilized as a means to preventing the birth of babies into poverty, we could rather alleviate poverty. This would ordinarily lead, after some delay, to a reduced birth rate. There are a number of problems with this argument. First, limiting reproductive freedom is often the only means of preventing harm to those who would otherwise be born into horrendously deprived circumstances. Poverty alleviation will take too long to save some potential people from this fate. Second, eliminating poverty, if this can ever be fully achieved, is much more difficult than encouraging people to be sterilized. Thus although it may not carry the cost of interfering with reproductive freedom and may be more desirable on these grounds, its greater difficulty and costliness may sometimes make the alternative greater interferences with reproductive freedom preferable. Third, poverty alleviation may sometimes be aided by curbing the birth rate. One of the reasons why it is so difficult to alleviate poverty is that the problem keeps growing on account of the tendency to a higher birth rate among those people in conditions of poverty. If we linked poverty alleviation to more direct efforts to curb reproduction, perhaps by prioritizing access to housing, education, and healthcare for those who limit their fecundity, we might more successfully solve the longer term problem while also effectively preventing harm in the short term.

Defenders of an extensive and muscular right to reproductive freedom may object that interfering with reproductive freedom, even where this is necessary to prevent serious harm, is unfair to those, such as the poor, the HIV-positive, and the carriers of genetic conditions, who, often through no fault of their own, find themselves in these unfortunate circumstances. The argument is that they are doubly disadvantaged. First, they are, for example, poor or HIV-positive. Second, and consequently, they would be deprived of the fulfilment of having children. Moreover, insofar as the rich bear some responsibility for the condition of the poor, the unfairness of imposing conditions on aid might be thought indecent.

There are a few responses to this argument. First, limitations on a right to reproductive freedom need not be unfair in the ways suggested. Thus, for example, any project to reduce the birth rate of the poor might provide for incentives to sterilize those who want children only after they have had two children but before they have many more. If such a project were linked to the provision of social services that would increase the chances of those children surviving, then the birth rate could be reduced without depriving the poor of the experience of parenthood. Indeed, the birth rate might be reduced to what the poor would choose if poverty were not influencing their procreative conduct. Second, procreation is not the only means to the fulfilment of parenthood. Adoption, although not without its difficulties and a distinct second-best for most people, can nonetheless afford carriers of genetic disorders the opportunity to rear children and thus to secure the fulfilment of interests in parenting. Finally, we can concede that there will be some circumstances where the application of my arguments will entail that those whose reproduction would be risky or harmful would be deprived of the opportunity to become parents. We might even concede that this is unfair, at least in the sense that it is unfair that they have a condition that makes procreation morally problematic. This unfairness has to be weighed against the unfairness of allowing them to produce children who will suffer terrible fates. Consider an analogy. It may be unfair that a person suffers from extremely drug-resistant tuberculosis and thus unfair that he finds himself with a condition that requires quarantine, but it would be still more unfair to allow him unrestricted freedom of movement that would result in the infection of new innocents. Similarly, a focus only on the unfairness to the potential procreators ignores the unfairness to those they would bring into existence.

In conclusion it must be emphasized that, although I have been critical of an expansive and very strong right to reproductive freedom, I should not be misconstrued as arguing either for its abandonment or for ham-handed curtailment. Instead, I have recommended a very careful and nuanced reconsideration of the right. It is an important right, but it is not the only important moral consideration. Preventing the existence of those who will suffer or stand a significant risk of serious harms is a sufficiently important moral consideration to warrant some limit on a right to reproductive freedom. Limiting this right, I have shown, does not usually involve physically forcing people not to reproduce, although it may, in the most extreme cases, involve this. Much more commonly it will involve lesser interferences with reproductive freedom.[25]

[25] I am grateful to David Archard and Jack Ritchie for helpful comments.

5

The Obligations and Responsibilities of Parenthood

DAVID ARCHARD

Consider the following four scenarios:

- John and Mary are in a long-standing loving relationship. Both of them want a child; to that end they engage in unprotected procreative sex at those times of the month when the chances of conceiving are highest. Mary has a normal pregnancy and gives birth.
- George and Sarah have a casual one-night stand. Both George and Sarah use contraception. George made it absolutely clear that he had no desire for a committed relationship with offspring. Nevertheless Sarah falls pregnant and decides to have the child.
- Frank is in a long-term relationship and has fathered two children now grown-up. Wanting to help infertile couples to experience, as he has, the joys of parenthood he becomes a registered gamete donor at a licensed fertility clinic. His gametes are used to create several children for different couples.
- Jean-Jacques Rousseau and his mistress, Thérèse, had five children, all of whom they deliberately abandoned at the gates of a nearby foundling hospital.

On what one might call the simple causal theory each of the men in these very different scenarios should bear parental responsibilities.

They should do so because they caused the child or children in question to come into existence. Such a theory has, as we shall see, much to commend it. Yet a widely shared intuition will be that whilst John, undoubtedly, and Jean-Jacques, almost certainly, has such responsibilities, it is far less clear that George and Frank do. My intention in this chapter is not to defend the causal theory but to show why it makes sense to say both that one has caused a child to exist and that one, nevertheless, is not always obliged to rear the child one has created. My principal interest will be in the idea that one might discharge a parental responsibility by making provision for others to care for the child.

The structure of the chapter is as follows. First, I will distinguish two senses in which one could speak of the duties of parenthood. Second, I will show why the causal theory is a theory of parental obligation and not a theory of parental rights. I will do so by criticizing what I shall term the 'parental package' view. Third, I will display the reasons for thinking that the causal theory of parental obligation is an attractive one whilst acknowledging the most obvious difficulties facing the theory. Fourth, I will make more precise the source and the content of the obligation that is incurred by the procreative act. Fifth, I will say something about the differences between the cases of George and Frank. Sixth, I will show how the argument thus far allows, without any ground for moral complaint, that a child might be reared by someone who did not cause the child to exist. In effect, I will defend the permissibility under some circumstances of child abandonment.

I

It helps at the outset to distinguish two senses in which one might speak of the duties of parenthood. These are not carefully distinguished in the literature on parenthood. There is an obligation to ensure *that* someone acts as a parent to the child, and there are the responsibilities of *acting as a parent*. One might term the first the 'parental obligation' (or, more accurately perhaps, the 'child-rearing obligation') and the second 'parental responsibilities'. The causal theory is a theory of how one comes to be under the parental obligation. According to the causal theory, causing a child to exist is a necessary condition of being under the parental obligation; according to what one might term the simple causal theory it is also a sufficient condition of one's being under that obligation.

The parental responsibilities need not be discharged by whosoever is under the obligation to ensure that the child is parented. But such responsibilities are those of ensuring that, as far as can reasonably be assured, the child is brought up sufficiently well. These responsibilities extend throughout the child's minority inasmuch as continuous care is essential to the well-being of the child. Thus, once someone has taken on the responsibilities of acting as a parent they should continue to do so unless there are good or unavoidable reasons for stopping.

The causal theory is not a theory of how someone might come to take on parental responsibilities. Of course someone who caused a child to exist might choose to discharge their parental obligation by assuming and fulfilling parental responsibilities. But that, as I shall argue later, is not necessary. Thus someone who had not caused the child to exist could act as the child's parent. He might assume parental responsibilities by an explicit declaration of intent to do so (as is the case in adoption) or by what could reasonably be inferred from his actions. Consider, as an example of the latter possibility, that someone finds an abandoned child, fails to identify its parents, takes it home, and cares for it.

I will here simply assert that those who take on parental responsibilities may do so only when no one else has a better claim to so act. This will cover cases of an orphaned child whom no one but a particular couple wish to parent through to complex disputed custody cases. The phrase 'better claim to so act' also leaves it open whether such a claim is to be grounded in a theory of parental rights, in an appeal to the best interests of the child, or in broader social considerations, or some combination of these. These matters need more discussion than can be given here. However since my principal concern here is with the parental obligation I will set them aside.

II

Recent philosophical work on parenthood starts from the assumption that it is in virtue of standing in a certain relationship to a child that adults have rights over and owe duties to that child.[1] Theories of the provenance of parental rights and duties include the causal, the genetic, the gestational, and the intentional.[2] Much of this work endorses a view that I reject.[3] The 'parental package view' holds that both parental obligations and rights in respect of any particular child somehow come as a whole 'package'. In fact for present purposes I will distinguish three versions of the view.

A failure to distinguish between 'parental obligation' and 'parental responsibilities' leaves it ambiguous as to which of the two it is that may come packaged with parental rights. I shall be criticizing the view that the parental obligation and parental rights go together as the 'parental package view' alleges. The first two versions of the 'parental package view' are about the parental obligation. The third version can be interpreted as about either parental responsibilities or the parental obligation.

The first version of the 'parental package view' is about how the parental obligation and parental rights are *acquired*. The particular version I shall criticize is:

(A) The facts in virtue of whose truth someone acquires a parental obligation are also those in virtue of whose truth that same person acquires parental rights.

---

[1] I will use 'duty' and 'obligation' interchangeably, reserving the term 'parental responsibilities' for what is required of someone who acts as a parent.

[2] The basic taxonomy of accounts of parenthood is due to Tim Bayne and Avery Kolers. See, for instance, their 2006. For a good critical survey of the possibilities, see Austin, 2007: esp. chs. 2 and 3.

[3] Someone who does criticize the view is Austin, 2007: ch. 3.

The second version of the parental package view holds that both the parental obligation and parental rights must always go together in the same person. The version I shall dispute is:

(B) Anyone who has a parental obligation in respect of a particular child will also have parental rights in respect of that child.

Claims (A) and (B) are false. The important general reason for the falsity of (A) is that rights and obligations have different kinds of ground. What gives someone obligations towards X would not necessarily suffice to give them any rights in respect of X. In the present context we can see this by imagining a case in which what gives rise to a parental obligation will not also give rise to a parental right.

The rapist whose victim conceives and gives birth is such a case. In virtue of causing a child to exist he incurs an obligation but he does not acquire rights over that child. He clearly has obligations to compensate the woman for the harm he does by the rape but he also has a parental obligation: he ought to ensure that the child is adequately provided for. This duty of adequate provision is not one owed to the mother even though its discharge may benefit her. Since he has no parental rights he cannot decide how the child is brought up. Moreover, given the circumstances of her pregnancy, it would be for the woman to determine how he should discharge his obligation. It would be reasonable for her to insist that he have no contact with her or with the child but that he should make proper financial provision for the child. Once again, this would mean payment to her of money not in reparation for the rape but to ensure that the resultant child could be satisfactorily brought up. The case of the rapist also shows (B) to be false. As would that of an abusive parent who loses custody of and even access to his child but is still required to make provision for that child. He is under a parental obligation but has no rights in respect of his child.

The claim that parental *responsibilities* and parental rights come as a package has some plausibility. Indeed the priority thesis defended by Jeffrey Blustein[4] can be interpreted as an interesting version of the package view. According to this thesis what it is for someone to have parental rights is specified in terms of morally prior parental responsibilities. A parent can choose for his child, and exclude others from the making of these choices, only in the service of and thus constrained by a duty to care for the child. It is in the first instance because a dependent child must have decisions made for it that a designated parent is entitled to make those decisions.

In this vein the third version of the parental package view maintains that parental rights and *responsibilities* go together as a *total* package. We start by noting that there is not a single parental right but rather a cluster of rights; there are also various parental responsibilities. This version then asserts that:

(C) If someone has both some parental rights and some parental responsibilities then they have all of the parental rights and all of the parental responsibilities.

(C) is a claim about parental responsibilities not the parental obligation. Claim (B) is false and the case of the abusive parent shows it to be so. Thus someone could have a parental *obligation* but no parental rights in respect of a child. However, claim (C) asserts, *if* someone has both *some* parental rights and *some* parental *responsibilities* then they must have them *all*.

Yet an abusive or neglectful parent might retain *some* of his parental rights whilst still being under the full parental *obligation* to ensure that the child is reasonably cared. He might also have those limited parental rights—for instance to make *some* decisions about the child conjointly with the mother—yet have no parental *responsibilities* inasmuch as he was not permitted to take care of the child.

For my purposes it is enough that (A) and (B) are false. An account of the origin of the parental obligation can be given that

---

[4] Blustein, 1982: 104–14.

is entirely independent of an account of the origins of parental rights. The falsity of these versions of the 'parental package view' disarms a type of argument that takes the following form. Facts of a certain kind—for instance, that P caused a child to exist—cannot serve as a ground for parental rights. Therefore, those facts cannot then serve as a ground of parenthood where this encompasses *both* parental rights *and* the parental obligation. Therefore, further, those facts cannot serve as a ground of the parental obligation. However if an account of the origin of the parental obligation can be specified independently of an account of the origin of parental rights, then this conclusion does not follow. What embarrasses an account of parental rights need not embarrass an account of the parental obligation. Thus a defender of a causal theory of parental obligation is free to criticize a causal theory of parental rights.

A very important reason to do so is that the idea that one has rights over that which one has created is essentially proprietarian. Proprietarianism in respect of children appeals to few.[5] Moreover the implication that a child should fall within the scope of that which having been created is thereby owned by its creators is discomfiting to any more general proprietarian theory. John Locke, famously, tried to show, with an ineptitude that Robert Nozick neatly exposed, that although parents do create children they do not own them as they would anything else with which they might have 'mixed' their labour.[6] But—to repeat—a causal theory of parental obligation leaves it open whether and why someone who has such an obligation also has parental rights.

---

[5] Defenders of parental proprietarianism include Aristotle: 'for the product belongs to the producer (e.g. a tooth or hair or anything else to him whose it is)'. *Nicomachean Ethics*, 8. 12. 1161b. In the contemporary period, see Narveson, 1988 and 2002; Hall, 1999.

[6] Locke's arguments for exempting children from his general proprietarian thesis can be found in *Treatises of Government*, bk. I, ch. vi, §§52–4. Nozick's critique of Locke's arguments can be found in Nozick, 1974: 287–9.

III

Why is the causal theory a plausible theory of parental obligation? First, the alternative accounts seem implausible. Second, it captures a widespread common-sense understanding of how one acquires an obligation in respect of a child. I shall not here rehearse the difficulties for the intentional, genetic, and gestational accounts. These are well described elsewhere.[7] I shall instead say something about the causal theory's credibility.

The first scenario of the four cited at the outset will strike everyone as a paradigmatic case of individuals knowingly and deliberately bringing it about that there is a child and, in consequence, having an obligation to ensure that the child is cared for. Of course the scenario is one in which the couple create the child intending to, and content that they should have to, discharge the responsibilities of parenthood. But the point is that having created the child they could not then renege on their obligation. As Judith Jarvis Thomson writes:

If a set of parents do not try to prevent pregnancy, do not obtain an abortion, and then at the time of the birth of the child do not put it out for adoption, but rather take it home with them, then they have assumed responsibility for it, they have given it rights, and they cannot *now* withdraw from it at the costs of its life because they *now* find it difficult to go on providing for it.[8]

What is it about the actions of John and Mary that warrant the ascription to them of this obligation? It is that they bring it about that there is a weak, dependent, and vulnerable human being who will suffer harms, and most probably die, in the absence of the care and protection that only adults can provide. The care and protection ought to be provided by those who are responsible for the child's state. In support of this basic idea Henry Sidgwick writes:

[7] See Kolers and Bayne, 2001; Bayne 2003; Bayne and Kolers, 2006; Austin, 2007.
[8] Thomson, 1971: 65.

'For the parent, being the cause of the child's existing in a helpless condition, would be indirectly the cause of the suffering and death that would result to it if neglected.'[9] In turn Sidgwick's thought echoes a much earlier comment from Sir William Blackstone who also stressed that the 'proper act' of procreation thus generates a clear obligation:

The duty of parents to provide for the *maintenance* of their children is a principle of natural law; an obligation, says Pufendorf, laid on them not only by nature herself, but by their own proper act, in bringing them into the world: for they would be in the highest manner injurious to their issue, if they only gave the children life, that they might afterwards see them perish. By begetting them therefore they have entered into a voluntary obligation, to endeavour, as far as in them lies, that the life which they have bestowed shall be supported and preserved.[10]

I will say more in due course about exactly what is meant, and what is entailed, by what I have simply called 'the child's state', and what Sidgwick describes as 'the child's existing in a helpless condition'. But at this point it is important to emphasize that the central idea motivating the causal theory is that it is reasonable to hold liable for the provision of care to the child those who have brought it about that there is a child in need of such care. Thus the causal theory both identifies those who incur this liability and specifies the scope of that liability, namely to rescue the child from its 'helpless condition' by the provision of care and protection.

The causal theory faces two obvious kinds of difficulties. First, how, in a manner that is neither arbitrary nor question-begging, should we identify the persons who, in virtue of their causal role, are responsible for providing care to the child? Second, how should we deal with the cases represented by the scenarios of George and Frank, in which it might seem, unreasonably, that causing a child to

[9] Sidgwick, 1982: 249.
[10] Blackstone, 1979: bk. 1, ch. 16, p. 435.

exist is sufficient for the acquisition of the parental obligation? I will take each in turn.

The first set of difficulties threatens the casual theory from two sides. The theory is in danger of being both over-inclusive and under-inclusive in those it identifies as obligated as parents. If playing *some* causal role—which, however small, is nevertheless necessary for the creation of the child—is sufficient to ground a parental obligation, then a very large number of people incur obligations in respect of the child: the midwife, the obstetrician, nursing staff; and, in the case of fertility treatment, we would need also to list the fertility clinician, nurse, and laboratory technicians. Indeed we can easily lengthen the casual chain to include the dating agency that facilitated the first meeting of John and Mary; the hotel staff that helped make that weekend break such a romantic one; and so on. How should we limit the set of causally responsible agents?[11]

From the other side there is the danger that the causal theory of parenthood is under-inclusive. Thus someone might be thought to incur an obligation towards a child in virtue not of causing the child to exist but in virtue of causing the child to be in a helpless condition. Consider, for example, the assassin who orphans the child by killing its parents. Or, again, someone might be thought obligated to care for a child in virtue of being the only person able to care for the child. Consider, for instance, the castaway who discovers that he and a baby who is not his are the only survivors of a shipwreck. In both cases the parental obligation to make provision for the care of the child is arguably not be found grounded in the act of causing the child to exist.

This chapter cannot hope to resolve these difficulties. An adequate defence of a causal theory of parental obligation would require a full elaboration and defence of a general theory of causation and liability. However the following comments are in order.

First, it is a mistake to conflate the empirical or metaphysical question of the degree of causal influence (what or who played the

[11] Millum, 2008.

most significant role in bringing X about) with the normative question of the degree of moral or legal responsibility for X. Some writers speak of those who are 'primary and proximate' causes of a child's existence.[12] But they court the risk of simply reading off the degree of individuals' moral or legal responsibility for the child's care from the magnitude or salience of their causal contribution to its existence.

Certainly some have thought that those who play the greater role in creating a child thereby acquire a greater *right* to rear the child. John Locke, for instance, thought it clear that a mother's contribution to procreation was greater than the father's, and implied that this might grant her more 'Dominion' over the child.[13] Some feminists would argue that gestational facts are the basis for exclusive claims over the resultant child.[14] However it would be a mistake to think that obligations can be understood in the same fashion. Second, a causal theory of parental obligation is not required to resolve those very difficult philosophical questions concerning who played an *essential* role in creating this particular child, and which arise from debates around conditions of identity.[15] These problems arise only if competing parties—such as a gestational mother and gamete donors—make incompatible normative claims of parental custody. In that context it might matter that one party can claim, 'But it is I alone who am responsible for there being this unique child with her particular nature'. In the context of ascribing parental obligation all that matters is that we can identify who is causally responsible for there being a child in existence, and hence in need of care and protection.

Third, the plausibility of the causal theory of parental obligation lies, to repeat, in the underlying thought that whosoever is causally

---

[12] Austin, 2007: ch. 3.

[13] 'For no body can deny but that Woman hath an equal share, *if not the greater*, as nourishing the Child a long time in her own Body out of her own Substance,' *Two Treatises of Government*, bk. I, ch. vi, §55; emphasis added.

[14] Rothman, 1989; S. Feldman, 1992.

[15] Kolers and Bayne, 2001: 279–80.

responsible by their actions for the existence of a child is responsible for ensuring that the child does not suffer the harms that it undoubtedly will in the absence of proper parental care and protection. This underlying thought is consonant with a common-sense view of moral and legal responsibility for harms which grounds it in attributions of causal responsibility.[16] In the standard cases of procreation—those represented at the outset by the case of John and Mary—the causal theory identifies, simply and directly, those whom we should hold responsible for the care of a child and does so in virtue of the role they played in bringing a child into existence.

Fourth, my intention here is not to offer a full defence of the causal theory of parental obligation. Rather it is to do two things. First, it is to specify the scope of that obligation. My principal claim is that *if* someone *does* incur a parental obligation to make provision for a child they have caused to exist then he or she is not under a duty to provide that care themselves. Second, it is to show that a simple causal theory of parental obligation is not defensible if it holds that causing a child to exist is sufficient to incur the obligation. In other words, I deny that George and Frank (from the scenarios at the outset) are obligated to care for the children they have undoubtedly caused to exist. To this second set of problems for the simple causal theory I now turn.

According to a simple causal theory of parenthood George acquires a parental obligation even though he did not wish or intend to create a child, and took all reasonable precautions to avoid doing so. Frank, as a gamete donor, is causally responsible for the creation of several children. He too, according to the simple causal theory, acquires a parental obligation even though he donated in the confident expectation that others would act as parents.

---

[16] 'In the moral judgments of ordinary life, we have occasion to blame people because they have caused harm to others, and also, if less frequently, to insist that morally they are bound to compensate those to whom they have caused harm.' Hart and Honoré, 1985: 63.

The cases are interestingly different in ways that will be subsequently explored. However both can serve to illustrate a strict liability version of the causal account. Jeffrey Blustein, James Lindemann Nelson, and Daniel Callahan have all argued, in line with such a strict liability interpretation of the causal account, that being causally responsible for the creation of a child is sufficient to generate a parental obligation.[17] The strict parental liability interpretation of the causal account appeals to what might be known as a risky action principle. This states that if you engage in actions which you know or ought reasonably to know risk certain serious consequences then you incur obligations in respect of these consequences; and that you do so if those consequences are brought about by your action *even if* you took all reasonable steps to avoid the consequences.

The thought is this. When you engage in procreative acts you risk creating a child who will suffer and die unless cared for. Hence the obligation you incur is to take steps to avoid that death and suffering. This obligation is incurred even if you took all reasonable steps to avoid the outcome (by, for instance, using contraception or assuring yourself that your sexual partner was using contraception). The obligation is incurred—according to the risky action principle—because the risked outcome is so serious; further the obligation is incurred by that person who most evidently caused the outcome. The risked outcome is such that *someone* must take remedial steps to deal with it. Who else could this be but the person whose action produced the risked outcome?

Here are other familiar and supposedly comparable examples of risky actions and their consequences. Late at night with no one else around I knock down a pedestrian even though I was driving whilst sober, fully awake, with all reasonable care and attentive to my surroundings. I surely have an obligation to assist him by taking him to hospital or waiting with him until an ambulance arrives. I have this duty even though I am not at fault for his injuries but just

---

[17]   Nelson, 1991; Callahan, 1992; Blustein, 1997.

because I caused them, and risked causing them by driving a car. I serve someone food to which they are allergic even though I had no way of knowing this and had taken all reasonable steps to purchase, prepare, and to provide what I believed was a safe dish. Arguably I have a special responsibility to help the victim of my cooking, and this is incurred just because I did serve him the 'poisonous' food and even though I took all reasonable measures to avoid doing so. Here the duty would presumably be discharged, as with the knocked-down pedestrian, by providing medical assistance or by ensuring that it is provided.

In some constructions of the cases X causes the harm and X alone is able to provide appropriate relief. Thus Carrier imagines that the knocked-down pedestrian needs transfusions of a rare blood type that only you can provide.[18] In order to concentrate on what distinguishes the procreator from other similar cases I do not presume that only the person who brings the child into the world can provide it with appropriate care. Indeed it is important to my argument that this is not so.

IV

In this section, I will begin to meet the challenge presented by the scenarios involving Frank and George by clarifying the grounds and the scope of the obligation that is incurred by the procreative act. In section V, I will spell out the differences between the cases of Frank and George.

The obligation that is acquired by engaging in the risky procreative act is to ensure that the resultant child, should one be created, does not suffer the harms of not being cared for. Thus the strict parental liability interpretation of the causal account differs interestingly from other risky action claims. The harm befalls the child only if the child is not cared for. Sidgwick's language is notably

---

[18] Carrier, 1975: 398–9.

careful and conditional: 'the parent *would* be *indirectly* the cause of the suffering and death . . . *if* [the child] was neglected' (emphasis added). By contrast, in the cases of the careless pedestrian and allergic diner, the harms directly befall persons as a result of my risky actions. Clearly I can seek remedies for the injuries I have caused and thus I can alleviate their suffering. Nevertheless my actions—driving and serving food—are, in and of themselves, the causes of harm and suffering. I could only have avoided causing them by not getting into the car or by not serving the food.

Between the procreative act and the helplessness of the created child lies the possibility of terminating the pregnancy. At birth various arrangements could be made to guarantee the provision of suitable care by willing persons other than the procreator. In the cases of the pedestrian and the diner what generates the obligation is the direct production of the risked harms. In the case of procreation what generates the obligation is the performance of the risky action *and* a failure to take further steps to avoid the 'suffering and death' of the child that will follow if the child is born or if the child, once born, is not adequately cared for.

The obligation, then, that is incurred by the procreative act is one of ensuring that any child that is born is adequately cared for. It does not follow that this obligation can only be discharged if the procreative agent provides the care in question. The individual who creates the child that is in need of an upbringing does not have to be the one who rears the child. The obligation is discharged if the child is reared by someone able and prepared to do so. That might be the person who is causally responsible for the child existing, but it might be someone who that person can be assured will do the job. The following two quotations, and their emphasized words, endorse this important point. The first is from Onora O'Neill arguing against the idea of an unconditional procreative right; the second is from Jeffrey Blustein spelling out the implications of the causal account:

I shall argue that the right to beget or bear is not unrestricted, but contingent upon begetters and bearers having or making some feasible plan for their child to be adequately reared by themselves *or by willing others*.[19]

Since biological parents can do x, where x involves caring for their offspring themselves *or making provisions for others to do so*, and since x would prevent y, where y involves harm to a human being, the failure of biological parents to do x can be said to cause y.[20]

In sum: on the causal account if I cause a child to exist then I am under an obligation to ensure that this child is cared for but the obligation is discharged if the care is provided by someone who is willing to care for the child. The causal account holds that causing a child to exist is a necessary condition of the obligation to ensure that someone acts as a parent to that child. The responsibilities of caring for a child, acting as its parent, need not be discharged by whosoever caused the child to exist. Nevertheless, if the individual who caused the child to exist cannot make provision for anyone else to care for the child then he must discharge the responsibilities of parenting. The causal account, as has already been conceded, awaits a proper defence of how some may be identified as the 'primary and proximate' causes of the child's existence, and thus under the parental obligation.

V

In this section, I look at the morally relevant differences between the cases of George, the unwilling and unlucky father, and Frank, the gamete donor. There are, to repeat, two obvious ways to avoid being, by one's procreative acts, the indirect cause, as Sidgwick has it, of the child's helpless condition. The first is a termination of the

---

[19] O'Neill, 1979: 29.
[20] Blustein, 1982: 143.

pregnancy; the second is by taking steps to ensure that the child once born is cared for.

In the case of George and Sarah she falls pregnant even though they both took all reasonable steps to prevent conception. We further assumed that George had made absolutely clear his desire not to have children. On falling pregnant Sarah chooses not to terminate the unwanted pregnancy. Does George by his (risky) procreative act nevertheless incur the obligation of ensuring that the child is adequately cared for?

There are two lines of response. The first is to deny that George is under such an obligation. Appeal might be made here to the idea that George's actions could not be described, in familiar jurisprudential terms, as negligent or reckless. He did not intend to create a child; he also took all reasonable measures to ensure that his actions did not have this outcome. The causal account might then be further modified in the following manner. Only those who may be identified as the 'proximate and primary causes' of a child's existence *and* whose causal role is intentional, negligent, or reckless incur an obligation to ensure that the child is parented.

The second line of response is to concede that George is under the obligation in question, but to argue that this is discharged insofar as Sarah has taken on the responsibility of acting as a parent. Her decision to have the child, rather than to terminate the pregnancy, may be taken as an expression of a willingness and desire to act as a parent. Insofar as Sarah is able, on her own, to care for the child, George has no parental responsibilities.

There is a great deal to be said about the kind of case that the George and Sarah scenario represents. It broaches issues extending far beyond the present piece.[21] These principally concern the fairness or unfairness of an outcome in which a man escapes parenting duties that fall exclusively upon a woman. Relevant to resolving these issues is an assessment of the burdensome nature of

---

[21] For feminists holding, respectively, that the man should be held liable and that he should not be held liable, see Mills, 2001; Brake, 2005.

acting as a parent, the costs to a woman of terminating a pregnancy, and the asymmetry involved in according a fundamental reproductive liberty to women which denies men like George a say in whether the child of their procreative act is born.

I here offer two further thoughts that pull in opposing directions. The first is that the second line of response must rely on a strict liability interpretation of the casual account. Now there can sometimes and in respect of some actions be reasons to enforce strict liability that are of sufficient importance to outweigh concerns about the violation of natural justice. For instance, one might evaluate the relevant conduct as worthless or morally base, or evaluate the dispositions of the agent concerned as vicious.[22] But it is hard to see how the character and behaviour of the prudent man who takes all reasonable precautions to avoid pregnancy can be understood in these terms.

The second line of thought appeals to our intuitions about a modified version of the scenario in which Sarah dies in childbirth. If George is under no obligation as a result of his risky procreative acts to ensure that the child is adequately cared for then his situation would be morally no different in the modified scenario from what it is in the original scenario. The child is unlucky in being an orphan, but George bears no responsibility for his fate. If this seems the wrong way to understand the modified scenario then it may well be that George *is* under a parental obligation.

Turning to the case of Frank, whereas the prudent procreator does not intentionally participate in the creation of a child the gamete donor does. The scenario is constructed to allow that the donor can be reasonably assured that the resultant children will be adequately cared for by others. Whereas the prudent procreator takes reasonable precautions to ensure that a child will not be created, the responsible gamete donor acts in order that there

---

[22] For a discussion of the defensibility of a strict liability rape offence which considers these kinds of argument, see Huigens, 2005.

shall be a child but in the reasonable expectation that someone other than himself will take on the responsibilities of parental care.

Tim Bayne identifies, and endorses, what he terms the 'transfer principle': 'it is permissible to alienate one's parental responsibilities (over neonates) to another individual (or institution) as long as one has good reason to think that they will carry out those responsibilities adequately'.[23] On the account I have offered the donor does not alienate the obligation incurred by causing a child to exist. Rather he has discharged it by ensuring that willing others will take on the responsibilities of acting as the children's parents. However Bayne's formulation of the 'transfer principle' is helpful because the gamete donor must have 'good reason' for thinking that others will carry out the responsibilities of parenting adequately.

VI

In this final section, I rehearse and try to dispense with worries one might have about thinking that the parental obligation is discharged by effectively abandoning the child to the care of others.

In respect of the gamete donor it may be objected that the obligation of ensuring that a child is cared for is just too important to rely on the actions of others. The obligation to care for a child is a very weighty one since it concerns adequate care of a vulnerable human being throughout its dependency.[24] I can think of two distinct kinds of worry. One is epistemic and concerns the adequacy of one's assurance that the child will be well cared for. The more serious the consequences of getting it wrong the more important it is to be assured that one is justified in assuming that it will be done right. But even with that qualification, an organized social scheme of child adoption with an assured historic record of general success will surely meet the epistemic concern. Similar comments

---

[23] Bayne, 2003: 82.
[24] Benatar, 1999.

apply to well-regulated institutional mechanisms for gamete donation within a system of licensed fertility clinics.

The second worry concerns the character of someone who
alienates, even to willing others, the discharge of weighty responsibilities. Such a person may act without due regard for the seriousness of the duty.[25] There is no doubt that some individuals will act
casually in the assurance that others will take on the responsibilities
of caring for those they have brought into existence. Yet it is also
true that someone may act conscientiously in the light of a considered judgement that others will be good parents. Frank does not act
in the same irresponsible manner as a feckless procreator who
carelessly and casually creates children. Frank has himself reared
children, and he donates gametes with the morally serious aim of
allowing others to act as parents. He only donates within an
institutional context that provides him with a reasonable assurance
that the prospective parents of his biological offspring will be well
cared for.

This brings us neatly to the final scenario. Onora O'Neill begins
her piece on the right to procreate by citing disapprovingly the
behaviour of Jean-Jacques Rousseau and his mistress, Thérèse, in
abandoning at the gates of the foundling hospital the five children
they produced. Rousseau himself insisted in his *Confessions* that he
acted entirely properly. He cited his own inability to be a good
father in justification:

Never in his whole life could J.J. be a man without sentiment or an
unnatural father....in abandoning my children to public education for
want of the means of bringing them up myself; in destining them to
become workmen and peasants, rather than adventurers and fortune-
hunters, I thought I acted like an honest citizen, and a good father.[26]

---

[25] David Benatar speaks of someone who 'manifests a lack of seriousness about' his
weighty responsibilities, ibid. 177.

[26] Jean-Jacques Rousseau, *Confessions*, bk. VIII (1749).

If Frank acts reasonably in creating children he will not parent what if anything was wrong with Rousseau's actions? Rousseau abandoned his illegitimate offspring but he did so within a particular institutional context that made provision for abandoned children. The American social historian, John Boswell, offers a fascinating historical study of the practice of child abandonment in his book *The Kindness of Strangers*.[27] Boswell points out that the practice of abandoning children—exposing them in public places, giving them to churches, or, as Rousseau did, leaving them at the gates of foundling hospitals—has been a widespread, and in its earliest form, morally acceptable one.

For Boswell a decisive change occurred with the arrival of the foundling institutions at the beginning of the thirteenth century. Within a hundred years or so this new system mopped up all the abandoned children of Europe. The system was funded and operated by strangers. It was not good for the abandoned children, a majority of whom died within a few years of admission. In some times and places the mortality rate exceeded 90 per cent. I will thus quote Boswell's comment on the change as a final judgement on Rousseau's actions:

Abandonment now became an even greater mystery, hidden from the public behind institutional walls from which few emerged, walls that afforded little opportunity for . . . triumph over natal adversity. The strangers no longer had to be kind to pick up the children: now they were paid to rescue them. But because it was their job, they remained strangers; and the children themselves, reared apart from society, apart from families, without lineage either natural or adopted, either died among strangers or entered society as strangers. Mostly, they died: unkind fortune, twisting gentle intentions to cruel ends, finally united in the flesh of infants those fates which had hitherto been joined mostly in rhetoric—abandonment and death.

----

[27] Boswell, 1988.

Arguably Rousseau suffered the circumstantial moral bad luck of abandoning his children at a time when their likely fate was a very poor one.[28] Had he lived hundreds of years earlier his actions might well have led to his children leading a better life that they would have done under his highly imperfect guardianship. Indeed had this been the case he should not have been the subject of Onora O'Neill's censure for he would have made some feasible plan for his and Thérèse's children to be adequately reared by willing others.

Of course Rousseau's abandonment of his children is a long way removed from Frank's considered donation of gametes. Rousseau's overriding thought may well have been a concern to rid himself of the inconveniences of caring for his own children, and a fundamental lack of interest in what happened to them. Those who left babies out in public places had their selfish purposes equally well served by the baby's death as by its fortuitous adoption by conscientious others. Moreover even if he was right to judge willing others to be better placed to care for his offspring his procreative recidivism suggests a morally troubling carelessness. We might in his case have real worries about someone who does not even bother to try to discharge parental responsibilities.

Set these worries to one side. What is there still to be said against abandoning one's child to the care of willing others who may indeed be better suited to care for the child? Here are some possible answers that I find unpersuasive. First, it might be insisted that the parental obligation can only be discharged by taking on the parental responsibilities, thereby simply ruling out the permissibility of making provision for others to care for one's children. The thought might be that this amounts to a non-transferable penalty for the culpable action ('*You* created the child; *you* suffer the consequences'). However this presumes that the action *is* a culpably bad one. Rousseau behaved reprehensibly. He ought to have

---

[28] For the classic study of moral luck, see Williams, 1993; for the characterization of circumstantial moral luck, see Nagel, 1993.

known by the birth of the fifth illegitimate child what he was doing, and he ought to have known what the fates of foundling children were. But not all procreative acts are culpable in a way that warrants the argument. Anyway further work is needed to show that compelling the assumption of parental responsibilities is the best or most appropriate way to punish culpable acts of procreation. Better perhaps to fine or otherwise punish Rousseau than to compel his children to suffer what undoubtedly would have been his poor parenting.

A second claim is that only the person under the parental obligation can take on the responsibilities of parenting, in the sense of being placed to do so and competent to do so. But this is clearly false. Others can and do take care of abandoned children. Equally it is false that only the obligated individual can discharge the responsibilities of parenting in a manner that yields the best overall results. Even taking into account the putative interests of a child in being reared by her natural parents, the natural parent is not always the best person to rear his own children.

It might be argued, third, that it is unfair if someone else discharges burdensome responsibilities. However unfairness arises from burdens unwillingly incurred. If another person is only too willing to assume the responsibilities of caring for a child—to the extent even of not seeing these as burdens—then where is the unfairness? Care is needed here. Adoptive parents may indeed want to care for those children whom their natural parents do not want or cannot care for. However we would be right to be troubled if those who become adoptive parents act only from an imperfect duty to care for those children whom others abandon. This amounts to the exploitation of the morally righteous by the morally weak or vicious. There is an interesting question concerning the fairness of compelling the performance of duties that arise only because of the failure of others to do theirs. For example, if it is for X to provide means of subsistence to Y, and he fails to do so, then arguably others are under a duty to save Y from the harmful consequences of X's failure.[29]

However within the context of enlightened and conscientious child adoption the assumption of parental responsibilities is by 'willing others' and, moreover, is of a kind that probably benefits the children. Thus the continued feeling that there is a measure of injustice in any arrangement of adoption surely derives from some version of the first criticism: '*You* created the child; *you* suffer the consequences'.

A fourth thought is that institutionalized systems of adoption encourage feckless procreation. Insofar as Rousseau knew that someone would look after his illegitimate offspring he could and did thoughtlessly carry on producing children. There is some merit to this charge, and it is the number of Rousseau's abandoned children that causes concern. He seems to have repeated his errors in the knowledge that he could avoid their consequences. However this is not always the case. Moreover, as already stated, it is unclear that enforced parenting is the best way to discourage feckless procreation. It would surely be better to compel the payment of child support than to insist that someone acts as a parent.

A fifth thought is that permitting child abandonment in this fashion amounts to toleration and perhaps even encouragement of a more general dereliction of duties. This rests on a contentious empirical claim. Failure to do your duty in one domain does not always and in every circumstance lead to a general failure to discharge your obligations. Furthermore nothing in any justification of a system of child abandonment need encourage general dereliction of one's responsibilities.

Sixth, Rousseau lost out by failing to act as a parent to his own children. This may be true. But his declaration in his *Confessions*, if sincere, might suggest that he would not have. It is also true that his

---

[29] Henry Shue includes a duty to provide people with subsistence when others who were under the primary duty to do so failed to do so as a duty correlate with the right to subsistence. See Shue, 1996: 57.

children would probably have lost out by having him as a parent. Moreover, insisting that it is in the interests of individuals to be parents is a troublesome concession to paternalism or perfectionism, the more so if arrangements are made to compel the assumption of a parental role.

VII

I have been concerned to demonstrate the consistency of a causal theory of parental obligation—that those who cause children to exist thereby incur an obligation to ensure that they are adequately cared for—with what is, in effect, child abandonment, the institutionalized practices of allowing for others to act as parents to children they have not created. I have distinguished between the parental obligation to ensure that the child has a parent and the responsibilities of acting as a parent. I have argued that a causal theory of parental obligation can be defended independently of a theory of parental rights, and has much to commend it. Nevertheless the causal theory must meet the difficulties outlined in section III of supplying a non-arbitrary and non-question-begging account of who amongst those who caused a child to exist, and why only those amongst this set of persons bear responsibility for caring for the child.

Someone can discharge their parental obligation without caring for the child by making provision for, or relying upon the institutional provision of, care of the child by willing and capable others. Had circumstances been more favourable to the children abandoned by Rousseau, or had prospective adoptive parents offered a better home than his, then his actions would arguably have been not much more morally troubling than those of the conscientious gamete donor.[30]

[30] I am extremely grateful to David Benatar for incisive and helpful criticisms of earlier versions of this chapter; and to Avery Kolers, the OUP reviewer, for further suggestions for improvement.

6

Parental Responsibilities in an Unjust World

COLIN M. MACLEOD

Parents are commonly thought to have special and particularly strong moral responsibilities to their children. They are expected to devote special attention to securing the needs and advancing the interests of their children and to display a concern for the well-being of their own children that they normally need not and often should not display towards other children. There are, of course, limits to the ways parents may act in promotion of the interests of their children. Parents may not violate the basic rights of others merely in order to secure a valuable benefit for their children and they are not even required to place all of their children's interests ahead of their own in deciding how to act. So, strictly speaking, it is false to suppose that parents should always act literally in the best interests of their children. Nonetheless, within certain modest constraints fixed roughly by the legal and core moral rights of others, parents are typically expected to manifest much greater concern for their own children than they do for others. Parental responsibilities are instances of the general phenomenon of associative duties or obligations,[1] that is, specific duties that persons in a special relationship have to others in that relationship in virtue of distinct and presumptively valuable features the relationship. The

---

[1] Dworkin, 1986: 195–216.

associative duties arising out of the relationship of parenthood, as opposed to those grounded in shared nationality, culture, or religion, are frequently depicted as having particularly strong normative force and significance. Indeed, special parental responsibilities are frequently cited as paradigmatic and incontestable examples of associative duties.[2] Moreover, parents' duties to their children seem more important than associative duties grounded in friendship or nationality. In cases of conflict, my duties as a parent usually have a greater pull on me than my duties as a friend or duties to my nation. On this common conception, parental responsibilities are, as I shall put it, *strongly valorized*: parents think that their own families do and should 'come first' and that the limits on how they can and should advance the interests of their children are the modest ones rooted in the widely and conventionally recognized rights of others.

Despite the apparent intuitive attraction of the strongly valorized conception of parental responsibilities, there seems to be a troubling tension between it and considerations of distributive justice.[3] This tension can take many forms but here I focus on how morally sanctioned parental partiality rooted in a common conception of parental responsibility can collide with the achievement of justice for children. The basic difficulty is simply that parents seem morally authorized to exercise their responsibilities to their children in ways that impede or frustrate the achievement of justice. For example, some parents can provide special educational benefits to their children and thereby confer upon them an unfair advantage *vis-à-vis* other children in the pursuit of employment or social opportunities. In this sort of case, we encounter the familiar tension between the putatively legitimate parental prerogative to send children to elite private schools and the achievement of fair equality

---

[2] See e.g. Jeske, 1986; Scheffler, 2001.

[3] Samuel Scheffler (2001) discusses various facets of the relationship between associative duties and distributive justice. He focuses particular attention on assessing the force the 'distributive objection' to associative duties, namely that associative duties can disrupt a just distribution of benefits and burdens by permitting persons in special relationships to confer significant and unfair advantages on those to whom they are specially related.

of opportunity.⁴ The tension seems even more pronounced and disturbing in the context of global justice. By any reasonable standard of justice, it is a grave injustice that the basic needs of millions of children routinely go unmet. From the point of view of justice we have reason to attach special priority to ensuring that children's basic needs are met. It seems very likely that, at least in short and medium term, effective action to meet these needs will require significant resource transfers from the global rich to the global poor. Yet to the degree that special parental responsibilities are strongly valorized, we can expect parents in affluent parts of the world to *feel justified* in resisting (either explicitly or implicitly) the kinds of policies and resource transfers that achievement of even minimal standards of global justice require. Affluent parents may view acceding to the demands of global justice as entailing a violation of their legitimate associative duties to their children. If strong valorization is justified, there is a potentially tragic normative conflict between justice and legitimate parental responsibilities.

The objective of this chapter is to explore this tension and to explain why parental associative duties, though genuine, are not as forceful as commonly believed. In this way, I hope to partially defuse the perceived tragic normative conflict between the demands of justice and the duties of responsible parenting. More specifically, I will examine the ways in which acknowledgement of associative duties of parenthood can pose obstacles to the pursuit of global justice. I shall argue that, at least in our grossly unjust world, strong valorization of special parental responsibilities is problematic and misplaced. Although considerations of distributive justice may not always trump distinct and conflicting parental duties, some considerations of justice are relevant to fixing the parameters within which parental responsibilities can be legitimately exercised. As a result, the character of genuine parental associative duties is more complex than commonly assumed. Exploring this complexity allows us to see the crucial ways in which parental

---

⁴ See Swift, 2003, for an illuminating and detailed examination of this particular issue.

associative duties are weaker and more qualified than the strong valorization view allows. The chapter is organized as follows. First, I shall introduce some assumptions about justice that are important to framing a general tension between justice and parental responsibilities. Second, I will distinguish different interpretations of the source and character of parental associative duties with a view to illuminating the sense in which there may be a deep and potentially tragic normative conflict between justice and parental responsibilities. Third, I outline a partial justificatory basis of strong valorization of parental responsibilities. Finally, I argue that inattention to the character of the circumstances in which associative duties (and parental duties specifically) arise can lead to exaggerated assumptions about the permissible strength and content of parental duties of the sort reflected in the strongly valorized conception of parental responsibilities. I maintain that the limits on parental responsibility are not fixed by the existing scheme of conventionally recognized rights and entitlements and that consequently the modest constraint dimension of strong valorization is mistaken.

Framing the Tension between Parental Responsibilities and Justice

There is controversy about the precise contours of a satisfactory theory of distributive justice. Many theorists, myself included,[5] are drawn to some variety of cosmopolitan egalitarianism according to which persons have a presumptive claim to an equal share of the resources and opportunities created through various forms of social cooperation. However, for the purposes of this discussion, I shall not endorse any particular variety of global egalitarianism but I will assume the soundness of a broadly impartialist theory justice according to which justice requires attending to the basic interests and

---

[5] See Macleod, 2002, for an account of how liberal egalitarian distributive principles should be extended to children.

needs of all persons. This implies, I believe, that children, simply as distinct members of the human community,[6] have some distinct justice-based entitlements to resources and opportunities that are not mediated through their particular families or the nations, states, or communities to which they belong. Moreover, I shall assume that fidelity to an impartialist conception of justice entails at least some easily specifiable substantive requirements. In particular, I assume that all children have a justice-based entitlement to secure access to the resources, opportunities, and institutional structures which are requisite to meeting their basic needs (for example, to adequate food, shelter, clothing, healthcare) and to the development of their agency and moral powers. This conception of justice also gives rise to duties of justice held by individuals to act in ways conducive to the realization of justice. This is a minimalist construal of the demands of justice regarding children and is entirely commensurate with the commitments of even notable sceptics of global egalitarianism such as John Rawls and Thomas Nagel. Rawls, for instance, while rejecting a global difference principle holds that global justice includes a duty to assist 'burdened societies'.[7] Similarly, Nagel, while rejecting cosmopolitan egalitarianism, recognizes a 'minimum humanitarian morality' that includes duties to meet basic needs.[8] It is plausible to suppose that full justice actually requires much more than this—for example, that children's overall life prospects be equal or that they enjoy fair equality of opportunity.[9] However, it will be sufficient for our purposes to consider the ways in which parental responsibilities

---

[6] Whether or not children should be considered independent subjects of justice in the sense of being 'full persons'—i.e. rational, autonomous, or responsible agents—is not, in my view, crucial to sketching the minimal demands of justice regarding children. We have reasons to be concerned both with the basic welfare interests of children, qua children, as well as their interests in becoming mature moral agents. Children are more vulnerable to harm and more systematically dependent on others than most adults but this fact does not weaken or qualify their claim to be included within the ambit of a theory of justice. Indeed, if anything, it enhances the importance of so including them.

[7] Rawls, 1999: 106.

[8] Nagel, 2005: 131.

[9] For defences of cosmopolitan egalitarianism, see Jones, 1999; Mollendorf, 2002; Tan, 2004.

might be in tension with even a minimalist construal of justice. Presumably, if there is serious conflict in this case, the conflict will be even greater if the conception of justice we endorse is more comprehensively egalitarian and hence demanding.

I must also make clear some substantive assumptions about what fidelity to even a modest view of global justice entails. First, I assume that the minimalist conception of justice is not, even approximately, satisfied in our world.[10] Just why this is so and what are the most efficacious and feasible strategies for achieving minimal justice are, of course, complex questions about which I have little to say here. I shall, however, assume that the failure to meet all the basic needs of the world's poorest children cannot be attributed solely to local failures—for example, the adoption of irresponsible policies by local governments or by irresponsible inattention or neglect of children's needs by families or communities.

Second, I assume that it is within the power of affluent persons in the world, particularly citizens of Western democracies, to effect significant material improvements in the prospects of poor children. These improvements can be realized either by acting individually through private organizations or by acting collectively via government action or by some combination of private and public action. There are, consequently, duties of justice to undertake the relevant actions.

Third, I assume that, at least in the short and medium term, eliminating gross injustice is a zero-sum game: in order to meet the most basic needs of poor children, affluent persons (for example, ordinary well-off and middle-class citizens, not just the super rich, of Western democracies) will need to make non-trivial transfers of resources that will leave them worse-off (and the global poor

---

[10] Even though there have been some modest improvements in basic child welfare recently, the plight of the worst-off children remains grim along many dimensions. According to UNICEF, 2008: 1, for instance, 'every day, on average more than 26,000 children under the age of five die around the world, mostly from preventable causes. Nearly all of them live in the developing world or, more precisely, in 60 developing countries.' No credible theory of justice, whether egalitarian or not, can view this as acceptable.

better-off) than they would be in the absence of action that has a significant impact on meeting the needs of children. In other words, affluent persons who contribute (either individually or collectively) to the realization of minimal global justice can expect a drop in the standard of living to which they are accustomed. These assumptions amount to the view that (*a*) we live in an unjust world, (*b*) that there are actions available to us to significantly reduce injustice, and (*c*) pursuing justice has costs for the affluent. I do not think these assumptions are particularly controversial. (It might, of course, be comforting for those of us who are affluent to think that one or more of them are mistaken.) But whether or not they are true is not crucial to the analysis. All that matters is that they could be true because the issue I wish to explore is how we should understand parental responsibilities in such a world.

Although I have so far referred solely to the special duties or responsibilities of parenthood, the conception of parental responsibilities at stake here actually involves both duties and prerogatives. The prerogatives of 'responsible parenting' take the form of moral permissions held by parents to advance the interests of children in ways that go beyond their obligations to their children. For instance, even if parents are not duty bound to send their children to the very best schools available to them, it is frequently assumed that parents may, if they so choose, provide their children with enhanced and advantage conferring educational opportunities. They are permitted to do so, even if such expressions of parental partiality create (either directly or indirectly) inequities between children. Of course, parents vary in the degree to which they exercise the prerogatives to confer extra benefits and opportunities on their children but it is widely assumed that 'good' parents do more than merely discharge their basic parental obligations. They also exercise the prerogatives of parenthood quite expansively. Thus affluent Canadian parents not only mark and celebrate the birthdays of their children, they also often buy them lavish and expensive gifts. (In the normal case, parents who decided to buy their children modest gifts and donated the money they would have spent on more expensive gifts to Oxfam do not, I assume, violate a duty to their children.) Although such expressions of parental partiality are not strictly speaking special parental duties, I shall, for the purposes of discussion, include them under the general heading of parental responsibilities. Responsible parents have distinct and special duties of care, attention, and affection towards their own children and they are motivated to exercise the special prerogatives of parenthood in ways that enhance the well-being of their children.

Against this background, a general tension between parental responsibilities and duties of justice seems fairly evident. The assignment of responsibilities to parents provides powerful incentives for parents, particularly in affluent Western states, to systematically privilege the interests of their own children at the expense of poor children. Wealthy parents will devote more time, energy, attention, and resources to caring for their own children than they do to meeting the needs of distant poor children with whom they have no special intimate relationship. Moreover, affluent parents will be motivated to secure and protect policies and institutional arrangements that are conducive to the promotion of their children's interests. They will resist policies they view as worsening the prospects of their own children (for example, substantial increases in the resources devoted to aid and development policies that are funded via increased taxation). So responsible parents—that is, those who take their special duties to their own children seriously—are likely to be at least reticent about reducing the range of benefits and opportunities available to their children even if doing so contributes to meeting minimal demands of global justice.

Diagnosing the Tension between Parental Responsibilities and Justice

The depth and seriousness of this tension, along with the prospects for its resolution, depend on how we understand its underlying sources. To begin with, we should note two different rationales for assigning special responsibilities to parents. The special duties of parenthood can be interpreted as either *pragmatic* associative duties or as *pure* associative duties.[11] Pragmatic associative duties are duties persons have to particular others, especially those to whom they have some special relationship, that arise because the most feasible means of achieving an impartialist moral standard is through the assignment of associative duties to persons occupying certain social roles and positions. For instance, we may agree that justice requires meeting the basic needs of all children but think that the best way to realize this demand is to assign special responsibilities to parents for the meeting of these needs.[12] If parental responsibilities are pragmatic associative duties then there can be no fundamental normative conflict between justice and parental responsibilities because parental duties are warranted only to the degree to which they actually serve justice. Of course, the assignment of special duties to parents may, as I explain below, give rise to unanticipated and unintended psychological and political obstacles to the fulfilment of duties of justice. These obstacles may be very difficult to overcome but they can be mitigated and perhaps even eliminated, at least in principle, by a suitably refined assignment of duties. Pure associative duties, by contrast, are duties that are intrinsic to certain valuable relationships and they have force in virtue of the fact and

---

[11] This distinction is similar in some respects to the distinction drawn by Scheffler between reductionist and non-reductionist accounts of associative duties. An interesting issue arises that I do not discuss: whether or not associative duties are voluntarily incurred (Scheffler, 2001: 98–100). Scheffler rejects a voluntarism while Jeske (1986) defends a complex variety of voluntarism. There is also a parallel here to the distinction, frequently made in discussions of utilitarian and consequentialist ethics, between direct and indirect forms of utilitarianism or consequentialism. Mill's utilitarianism is plausibly interpreted as a variety of indirect utilitarianism precisely because he allows that the best way for agents to manifest fidelity to the impartial utilitarian criterion of rightness (of maximizing overall happiness) is to be guided by a decision procedure that acknowledges and responds to considerations of partiality such as love, friendship, and self-interest. The best division of utilitarian moral labour, so to speak, is one that permits and encourages agents to display partiality but this is not because partiality has moral force that is independent of the utilitarian standard of rightness. Rather, partiality is employed in service of the impartial principle of utility. Peter Railton's (1984) influential variety of 'sophisticated' consequentialism has a similar structure.

[12] Martha Nussbaum seems to endorse a pragmatic account (1996: 135).

value of these relationships, not because they are instrumental to serving other moral aims such as justice. Here the normative force of pure associative duties is located in values distinct from justice. The possibility that there is a tragic normative conflict between parental duties and duties of justice depends on treating parental duties as pure associative duties. But before we examine this possibility more closely, we should note two non-normative ways of diagnosing the general tension between justice and parental duties we have observed.

First, the tension might be largely psychological. In order to be appropriately responsive to the full range of children's needs, parents need to be attentive to the distinctive attributes of particular children. Although we can care in a general and diffuse way about the well-being of all children, it is psychologically taxing and probably impossible for parents to respond to the idiosyncratic needs and preferences of children in general. Instead, we form close, powerful, and rewarding bonds with particular children and we become strongly psychologically motivated to advance those to whom we are intimately related. The psychological tendency to respond to and promote the interests of intimates and consequently to be less aware of and responsive to the needs (or entitlements) of others does not directly imply anything about the relative normative force of parental responsibilities and duties of justice. The point here is that there can be psychological obstacles to integrating parental responsibilities with duties of justice. In an unjust world, the psychological tendency to focus attention on one's intimates may distort our moral perception of, and our motivation to respond to, the legitimate claims of distant others.

Second, the tension can have a political dimension in the sense that the assignment of special responsibilities to parents may tend to generate collective action failures that require specifically political solutions. However, in the absence of suitable, justice-friendly, political arrangements the tension between parental responsibilities and justice is exacerbated. For example, from a collective point of view all parents might acknowledge the importance of securing the

minimal demands of justice for all children and they might consequently prefer the adoption of policies to realize justice, even if
such policies impose constraints on the benefits that they can confer
on their own children. However, affluent parents will be reluctant
to sacrifice the pursuit of benefits for their own children unless they
have suitable assurances that other affluent parents will abide by the
requisite constraints. Thus most parents might believe that children
should enjoy equal educational opportunities and might be in
favour of the abolition of elite, advantage-conferring private
schools. But if private schools exist and some affluent parents send
their children to them then even parents who favour the elimina-
tion of private schools may feel compelled to send their children to
such schools because they fear that their children will be disadvantaged in relation to the children who do attend such schools.[13]
Similarly, at the global level parents might favour the adoption of
redistributive policies providing they are adopted (in an equitable
fashion) by all wealthy states. But in the absence of assurances that
other states will adopt the relevant policies, parents will not lend
political support to the unilateral adoption of redistributive policies
by their state that generate comparative disadvantages for their
children *vis-à-vis* the children in other wealthy states.[14] The assignment of special responsibilities to parents may tend to lead to these
types of collective action failures but this does not mean that
parental responsibilities and duties of justice cannot be harmonized.
The difficulty is that they can only be fully and reliably harmonized

---

[13] Swift, 2003: 96–113.

[14] I do not want to overstate the force of this explanation for the lack of political support
for global redistribution policies since many factors, including false beliefs of citizens about
the levels of aid currently provided by states, are relevant. For instance, as Jeffrey Sachs (2005:
329) notes: 'the American public greatly overestimates the amount of federal funds spent on
foreign aid. In a 2001 survey, the Program on International Policy Attitudes (PIPA) at the
University of Maryland reported that Americans, on average, believed that foreign aid
accounts for 20% of the federal budget, roughly twenty-four times the actual figure.' Still
this suggests that one source of American resistance to increasing foreign aid is the belief,
deeply false though it may be, that the USA already contributes a lot and probably propor-
tionally more than other affluent states.

through the adoption of political measures that are, given the conflicting incentives of actors in an unjust world, elusive.

I suspect that these psychological and political forces are significant factors in the phenomenon of strong valorization of parental duties I noted at the outset. Parents are psychologically and politically primed to privilege the interests of their own children and to *feel* vindicated in doing so. This can be so even if, as a matter of moral theory, parental duties are viewed as pragmatic associative duties. Of course, this does not provide normative warrant for exercising parental responsibilities in ways that conflict with the realization of justice. Strong valorization may be explainable without being justified. So the issue we must address now is whether strong valorization has a credible normative justification.

Pure Associative Duties and Strong Valorization

Let's first take a closer look at the general idea that parental duties are pure associative duties. The basic idea is that the normative source and character of parental duties (and associative duties more generally) and duties of justice are distinct and when these duties conflict, as they inevitably do, the conflict cannot be definitively resolved by appeal to deeper values or higher order adjudicative procedures. On this view, something about the intimate relationship between parents and children permits and requires parents to devote special care and attention to the promotion of the needs and interests of their children in at least some ways that cannot be legitimately constrained by the requirements, particularly the demanding redistributive requirements, of impartial justice.

The responsibilities of parenthood are not boundless, of course, but they extend at least as far as is necessary to facilitate the integrity of intimate relationships and generous opportunities to express love, affection, and concern to one's family and to share with them meaningful projects and practices. Gift giving from parents to children provides a good illustration of the way parental responsibilities appear to have a normative authorization that is not (fully) constrained by justice. Affluent families often shower their children with expensive gifts as a way of expressing their affection in the context of shared family and cultural traditions (such as Christmas, Hanukah). Although parents often recognize that the money spent on these gifts could be directed to meeting the basic needs of distant children, they feel that promoting the happiness of their own children constrains what they can and should do by way of helping others. From this perspective, duties of global distributive justice (viewed either in individualistic or collective terms) seem excessively and unreasonably demanding.

The relationship between parents and children appears to have special normative significance because it is (or can be) a profound source of meaning for both adults and children. But it is doubtful that this normative significance is rooted in the brute fact of a close relationship. After all, close relationships whose purpose or orientation is the achievement of wicked ends are not credible sources of genuine associative duties. Thus the member of a close-knit criminal syndicate does not have a real duty of loyalty to remain silent about the murderous activities of fellow gang members merely because he stands in a close relationship to fellow criminals.[15] Genuine pure associative duties must be predicated on credible goods internal to close relationships. So an adequate justification of pure associative duties requires a somewhat fuller characterization of special goods that purport to justify special duties. Without developing a full account of 'family values', I think we can distinguish three distinct ways in which parenting is special locus of meaning and can furnish parents and children with important goods.[16]

---

[15] This is not deny, of course, that criminals may (falsely) believe that they have a duty of loyalty.

[16] Brighouse and Swift provide an account the value of family life that has some affinities with my account. Brighouse and Swift give special attention to the value of intimacy and the consequent interest parents have in realizing intimacy via distinctive elements of parenting. They seek to use the special interest parents have in intimacy in grounding a range of parental

First, intimacy seems important to parents and children. The historical and often biological links between members of the same family are often represented as a special source of meaning. Members of a family are inextricably entangled in the life narratives of those with whom they share family ties. Part of the challenge to which we must respond as a family member is provided by a (largely) unchosen family history we are presented with. It provides a kind of narrative framework or context of meaning. We find ourselves located in a web of close-knit relationships that present opportunities for interpretation and response. In families where there is a degree of successful integration, the intimate entanglement is a source of special obligations to other family members and the challenge of responding to these obligations assumes its own importance. In less successful families, members are alienated from each other and their shared history. Their close interpersonal connections do not resonate with them as a source of special meaning, obligation, or even as something worthy of appreciation.

Second, there is what I shall call cherishment. The family can also provide a context for receiving and expressing special and often intense love and emotional attention. Our relationships with family members, especially but not only children, are often marked by an experience of profound and pervasive emotional engagement. In good families, we cherish our family and are cherished by it. We seek appropriate ways to express and appreciate this cherishment. For example, how can we best display and communicate our special pride in our children? We also have reason to be receptive to feelings of awe and joy when witnessing different facets of development and achievement of one's family. And we try to experience and express our sorrow and disappointment suitably when misfortune or tragedy befalls our family. Families in which relations are

---

rights to raise children (Brighouse and Swift, 2006). My view endorses the value of intimacy but interprets its value as a wider relational good available to and important for families in general. I find their claim about the relation between parental interests in intimacy and parental rights plausible but my analysis here does not depend on accepting it.

characterized by indifference, emotional distance, or enmity cannot appreciate or respond to the importance of cherishment.

A third facet of the intrinsic value of family relationships, what I call creative self-extension, arises out of the special opportunity family members, but especially parents, have to express their own commitment to ideals and ground-projects by passing them on to children. Families often strive to create and maintain shared enthusiasms, projects, and interests. The pursuit and promotion of such commitments shapes the identity of children and is integral to the generation of a kind of familial unity or solidarity. The recognition that valued features of one's own sense of self have been extended to one's children and now form part of their sense of self can be a profound source of satisfaction. We can see ourselves carried forward in another self we played a significant role in creating.

Suppose we accept that the values of intimacy, cherishment, and creative self-extension can animate special parental responsibilities. This means that realization of these values is dependent on parents devoting special moral attention to their relationship with their children and that pursuit of these values is sufficiently important to provide normative warrant for such special attention. On the pure associative duties view, pursuit of these values is legitimate, at least to some important degree, even if doing so entails failing to fulfil duties of justice. This does not mean that parents are simply authorized to do whatever they can to realize such values to the maximum degree possible. We might instead think that there is some threshold of robust realization of the values that it is permissible and even desirable for parents to try to attain given the means at their disposal. But this can seem quite plausible. For example, suppose that meeting my justice-based duty to alleviate global poverty requires me, an affluent Canadian, to contribute $10,000 to Oxfam but that a donation of that size would frustrate my objective of realizing shared goods of intimacy, cherishment, and creative self-expression with my son. Perhaps my son will feel alienated from me if I devote a lot of resources to meeting the

basic needs of distant children. Also I will not be able to express my
cherishment of him by giving him distinctive gifts and the range of
activities and commitments that we can enjoy in the pursuit of
creative self-extension will be greatly diminished (for example, I
will not be able to travel with him to Scotland, India, and Israel to
explore our family ancestry). It may seem crass or shallow to
suppose that realization of such relationship values can be so dependent on the use of material resources.[17]

Although it is probably true that in affluent families there is too
much emphasis on material expressions of love, concern, and
commitment, I assume that adequate realization of relationship
values often has non-trivial material conditions. The crucial point
is that my pure associative duties as a parent can conflict with
duties of justice and this conflict need not be resolved in favour of
justice even if the goods realized fulfilment of duties of justice are,
when judged from an impartial perspective, more important that
those realized by fulfilment of parental responsibilities. Suppose my
donation can save the lives of a hundred children and secure for
them their basic needs without jeopardizing the basic needs of my
son. From an impartial perspective this seems more important than
my enjoying an especially rewarding relationship with my son. If, as
this artificial example suggests, relationship values can only reliably
be achieved by affluent parents by systematically prioritizing such

---

[17] The realization of relationship values also depends on the expenditure of time and
emotional energy. A successful family life requires parents to spend time with their children
and devote serious thought to the particular interests and emotional needs of their children.
But, at least to some degree, the time and energy devoted to cultivating and nurturing
relationship values can come at expense of engagement in political activity aimed at achieving
justice. So perhaps I should worry about playing tennis with my son when I could be at the
political rally or writing letters to the editor. And this might suggest that the crux of tension
between justice and parental duties is not the way affluent parents use material resources in
developing relationships with their children but how they spend their time on their children.
I agree that time matters both to rewarding parenting and to political activity concerned with
global justice but I am sceptical that contributing fairly to effective political activity is
particularly demanding in terms of time spent. I suspect that I can make a much more
significant contribution to political action by spending a few minutes cutting some large
cheques to the causes that I support than by devoting most of my spare time to marching in
rallies and the like.

values over the achievement of justice then there will indeed be a tragic conflict between parental responsibilities and justice. The conflict seems tragic because two genuine but different sources of value collide and cannot be simultaneously realized or respected without significant normative loss. Even if we allow, as I have been supposing here, that it is reasonable for parents to pursue familial goods at the expense of some considerations of distributive justice this does not mean that pursuit of familial values is itself authorized by justice, all things considered, or that the permissible pursuit of familial goods at the expense of justice should not occasion regret. A conflict between values can be tragic even if there is, in the final analysis, an acceptable way of prioritizing values.[18]

But the analysis thus far has not established that such a conflict is real or tragic, only that it is possible. Indeed, it remains possible that parental responsibilities and duties of justice are fully harmonious even if they have distinct normative foundations. After all, there is nothing incoherent about a world in which justice obtains and all parents discharge their responsibilities in the successful pursuit of intimacy, cherishment, and creative self-extension.

The issue we need to broach is the degree to which this harmony is achievable in our unjust world. The scope and gravity of the tension between justice and parental responsibilities (understood as pure associative duties) in our world is, I suggest, partly dependent on how we interpret the circumstances in which the duties arise. To get at this point, I now want to consider more closely what strong valorization involves and how it can yield an apparent tragic conflict between justice and parental responsibilities.

---

[18] Although the context is in important respects quite different, we can see this type of tragic conflict at play in the excruciating dilemma faced by the protagonist of William Styron's novel *Sophie's Choice*. Sophie is cruelly forced to choose between selecting one of her children to be spared from death and permitting them both to be killed. Even if we think she chooses correctly by selecting one to be saved, we can view the conflict between values she faces as tragic. It's deeply regrettable that she should have to face the choice and she can reasonably experience regret about how she chose, even if she chose correctly.

Strong valorization of parental responsibilities (and prerogatives) has two components. First, the achievement of relationship goods is celebrated as a nearly dominant source of normative commitments. (This is the 'family comes first' dimension.) Second, the only constraints on the exercise of parental responsibilities are those supplied the *de facto* juridical status quo, that is, by the distribution of resources and opportunities viewed as legitimate by prevailing political authorities and accepted in broad public sentiment. (This is the modest constraint dimension.) Within these fairly modest constraints, parents are encouraged to exercise their responsibilities in the manner most conducive to the promotion of valuable outcomes for their children and family as a whole.

Something like strong valorization of parental responsibilities seems to operate in the background of many discussions of associative duties. It is assumed that not only is it legitimate for persons to devote more care and attention to the interests of their families, friends, and co-nationals but that they may do so through use of material resources over which they have control and to which they have a presumed entitlement. And it is against this background that a tragic conflict between duties of justice and parental responsibilities will seem most pronounced. I may know that transferring a substantial portion of *my* income (that is, the income to which I have a clear legal entitlement and which is widely viewed as mine) to Oxfam will promote justice but I also see that I could use the income in ways that will enhance valuable dimensions of my family life and that I have, moreover, a responsibility do to so. Given the strong sentimental and psychological attachments I have to my own children (not to mention my own interests and the pull they exert on my behaviour) it is likely that I will resolve the tension to the favour my parental duties. Even if I acknowledge the legitimacy of duties of justice, I can, in the light of parental responsibilities, see my decision as morally warranted. If the achievement of the relationship goods I have sketched is profoundly important then we can perhaps acknowledge that there is independent normative warrant for their pursuit. So I will concede, for the sake of argument, that the family-comes-first element of strong valorization is credible. But the status of the modest constraint dimension of strong valorization is less clear.

To see this, it will help to make explicit two assumptions implicit in the foregoing analysis, namely there is variation in the degree to which relationship goods can be realized and that, at least to some significant degree, access to more resources and opportunities can facilitate fuller realization of these goods. This does not mean, of course, that affluent parents always have better relationships with their children than those who are less well off but it does suggest that affluence, at least to a point, tends to provide advantages in the pursuit of relationship goods.[19] It is certainly common for parents to express their concern for their children materially, namely by using their resources to confer benefits and opportunities on their children. But we need to take special notice of the way that the resource entitlements of others can limit the achievement of relationship goods. Thus even if taking my son on a trip to Scotland would deepen my relationship with him and allow us to achieve greater intimacy, I cannot finance the trip by stealing money from a stranger. I must either find a different, less expensive, way of realizing relationship goods or I must accept, as legitimate, a lesser, but still satisfactory, attainment of those goods than would be possible if I were richer.

The important point to recognize here is that in some contexts, the moral propriety of de facto ownership of resources is itself an important issue. But this point is arguably obscured by the modest constraint assumption in the strong valorization conception. We cannot merely assume that the existing property regime sets the parameters within which even pure associative duties may be legitimately exercised. This general point tells against acceptability of strong valorization. By way of illustration, consider first an

---

[19] If this were not so then affluent parents could not complain that redistribution might impede or frustrate the achievement of relationship goods.

obvious case in which the failure to critically challenge an existing property regime renders the exercise of parental responsibilities problematic. Imagine a slave owner who loves his children and seeks to express his devotion by conferring special advantages on them. One way in which he can do this by getting his slave to make special toys for the children and to create elaborate intimate family dinners. The slave owner's legal control of 'property' facilitates the achievement of relationship goods but surely we can challenge the permissibility of using another person as property in this way. Morally speaking, though it may be very difficult both psychologically and politically for him to do so, the slave owner should forgo the benefits that accrue to slave ownership. In this case the *de facto* legal constraints on exercise of parental responsibilities do not track the relevant moral ones.

It might be objected that injustice of the property holdings in the slave case have no parallel to the property regimes in place in affluent Western societies and hence that the example does not tell against the plausibility of the strong valorization in the contemporary context. Whereas slavery is an inherently unjust property regime that violates basic human rights, existing property regimes (though perhaps not perfect from the point of view of justice) are not corrupt and enjoy sufficient legitimacy to set the parameters for the exercise of parental responsibilities. This is not, however, enough to save strong valorization because a property regime, even if it is not inherently corrupt, can be tainted by various forms of historical injustice. One relevant possibility is that many citizens of affluent states are innocent inheritors of the benefits of the past injustice of colonialism and imperialism. It is plausible to suppose that some of the advantages that some people enjoy today (and the disadvantages others face) are traceable to the effects of blatant injustice involving the violation of basic human rights. If this is so then it is difficult to see why we should accept the current *de facto* distribution of property rights as setting the legitimate parameters within which parental responsibilities can be exercised.

The point here is not to argue that all duties of distributive justice must be discharged before parental responsibilities can be permissibly exercised. (That would be simply to reject the moral legitimacy of pure associative duties.) Rather it is to challenge the idea that the conventionally accepted juridical status quo provides an adequate specification of the constraints on parental duties. Put somewhat differently, the point is that strong valorization is not entailed by a pure associative-duty interpretation of parental responsibilities. Even on the pure associative-duty view, a more qualified valorization of parental responsibilities seems appropriate. It can acknowledge the high normative value of relationship goods and authorize their achievement. But it should be receptive to the possibility that the existing normative order lacks full legitimacy and that consequently that the moral constraints on exercising parental responsibilities may be more extensive than those reflected in the resource entitlements recognized by the status quo. In short, some ways of exercising parental responsibilities are morally problematic because they involve the use of resources and opportunities by parents whose full moral entitlement to the resources is suspect or tainted.

A tragic normative conflict between justice and parental responsibilities will seem to be a feature of our world if we attribute broad legitimacy to the property regimes endorsed by the juridical status quo. But we have reason to doubt the legitimacy of the status quo. Moreover the grounds for doubting its legitimacy do not rest on appeals to principles of cosmopolitan egalitarian distributive justice. We need only appeal to the long and ugly history of basic human rights violations and the fact that these injustices have shaped the share of resources and opportunities that people have today. It is difficult to determine what a genuinely legitimate global property regime would look like in detail but it does not seem implausible to suppose that it would eliminate the worst forms of deprivation that currently blight our world. And we can be cautiously optimistic that in such a world all persons could adequately pursue relationship goods without the necessity of depriving others of their just share of resources and opportunities.[20] The challenge for us, I believe, is to determine how to fix the parameters of parental responsibilities when we lack confidence in the parameters supplied by the juridical status quo. We may discover that some conflicts between duties of justice and pure associative duties remain even after more suitable and legitimate parameters are identified. But I suspect that greatest difficulties we face in reconciling justice and parental duties are psychological and political rather than normative. The difficulty is not that justice *per se* conflicts with parental responsibilities but that illegitimate property regimes exercise enormous influence over our psychological expectations and our sense of political possibilities. For those of us who benefit from the juridical status quo, a substantial reduction in our standard of living and a consequent reduction in the range of rewarding activities we can pursue with our families seem very daunting, especially when we have been encouraged to believe that we are justly entitled to the resources we currently enjoy. Resistance to addressing the illegitimacy of existing property regimes might be justified if changes to them rendered successful pursuit of relationship goods impossible or even extremely difficult. But we should be cautious about supposing that we can only satisfactorily pursue relationship goods with the share of material resources we currently have. If the obstacles to pursuing them in the context of a more legitimate property regime are more psychological and political than normative then we should not

---

[20] This does not mean that there would not be significant changes in the manner and degree to which relationship goods could be achieved. Affluent families would likely have to find different and more modest ways of realizing relationship goods and this might result in some genuine loss of value for them. However, providing that affluent families can still realize, with a fairer share of resources, the relevant goods to a sufficiently robust threshold, the tragic conflict between justice and parental responsibilities can be avoided. Settling for different and less extravagant modes of realizing relationship goods may be frustrating to those accustomed to expensive ways of manifesting intimacy, cherishment, and creative self-extension but it does not, I think, constitute a deeply regrettable normative loss. Changing one's habits and expectations in these matters may prove psychologically taxing but unless the psychological burdens are especially grave and excessive such demands do not justify abandonment of efforts to find more modest ways of fulfilling parental responsibilities.

invoke special parental duties as a justification for resisting some of the distributive dimensions of justice.

Conclusion

I have suggested that in our unjust world the putative normative tension between justice and parental responsibilities is more illusory than real. This is most apparent if parental responsibilities are pragmatic associative duties. The pragmatic associative-duties interpretation cannot justify strong valorization of parental responsibilities but it is compatible with the idea that assignment of special duties to parents can give rise to significant psychological and political obstacles to justice. Vindication of strong valorization depends on treating parental responsibilities as pure associative duties. I sketched a justificatory account of pure associative duties but argued that it fell short of justifying the modest constraint dimension of strong valorization. I should perhaps emphasize that some of the premises of the analysis are controversial and not fully defended here. In particular, I have not developed the idea that current property regimes bear the moral taint of various forms of historical injustice in ways that challenge the legitimacy of the juridical status quo. To be clear, my claim is not that the citizens of affluent Western nations are active participants or even complicit in ongoing unjust oppression. Rather my claim that we are all, in a sense, innocent inheritors of the legacy of historical injustice. Some of us are lucky enough to be the beneficiaries of this legacy. For others, including millions of deprived children across the world, the inheritance is dreadful. In determining what the legitimate parameters of parental responsibilities are, we should not confuse good luck with entitlement.[21]

---

[21] Thanks to David Archard and David Benatar for helpful comments.

7

Willing Parents

A Voluntarist Account of Parental Role Obligations

ELIZABETH BRAKE

Much of the bioethical literature on parenthood does not address a fact about parenthood which deserves more attention: parental rights and obligations are attached to socially constructed institutional roles. Both the content of these roles, and the way in which they determine who a child's parents will be, issue from social and legal institutions of parenthood, and this makes a difference to accounts of the moral basis of parenthood. I will argue that this poses a problem for the causal account of parenthood: the variability of parental obligations, and their assignment, underscores the problems the causal account has with defining the relevant notion of cause and with fixing procreative costs. If institutional role obligations arise only through voluntary undertakings, then understanding moral parenthood as an institutional role makes the voluntarist account of parenthood more attractive. However, I must address two questions: whether such role obligations can arise non-voluntarily, and whether the voluntarist account can account for commonly accepted cases of parenthood.

The Voluntarist Account

One version of the voluntarist account of parenthood, defended by Onora O'Neill, holds that a voluntary undertaking to procreate is sufficient for the acquisition of moral parental obligations but leaves open whether those obligations can be incurred in other ways.[1] In this chapter, I defend a stronger version of voluntarism: voluntary acceptance of moral parental obligations is necessary, but not sufficient, for such obligations. It is not sufficient because at least two other conditions must obtain: that those taking on the obligations be able to carry them out, and that the child be eligible to be parented by them.

The grounds of parenthood depend on the type of parenthood under investigation. To make my argument clearer, it is helpful first to distinguish legal, biological, social, and moral parenthood. A legal parent holds legal parental rights and responsibilities. Legal parents of a child need not be its biological parents, as in cases of adoption, gamete donation, and contract pregnancy. Biological parenthood is often contrasted with social parenthood, where the social parent actually rears the child. While social parents are usually legal parents, the concepts are not equivalent: a child can be transferred for a period to care-takers who are not its legal parents.

Moral parenthood is a further, conceptually distinct, sense of 'parenthood' (although whether necessary connections hold between this concept and the others is at issue in accounts of moral parenthood). An investigation into moral parenthood is an investigation into the moral grounds of parental rights and obligations. Biological parenthood need not bring moral parental obligations (standard examples are sperm donation or gamete theft), and legal parenthood can be wrongly assigned to someone with no antecedent moral parental rights or obligations.[2] Indeed, law may

---

[1] See O'Neill, 1979. Versions of this view are also referred to as the 'consent' account (see Austin, 2007: 34) and the 'intentional' account (discussed below).

[2] Law can ground moral obligations: legal assignment of parenthood may give the legal parent moral obligations, even if she had none beforehand, either because legal reasons

have different grounds for assigning parenthood than the strictly moral. The urgent need for legal assignment of child-care responsibility can draw legal and moral parenthood apart: moral grounds of parenthood might resist discovery (for example, if they involve psychological states) or involve a balance of considerations too fine for law to measure. As for social parenthood, we can conceptually distinguish those rearing a child as its parents, and putting themselves forth as its parents, from those holding parental moral rights and obligations.

The subject of this chapter is moral parenthood; that is, the question is what moral principles imply regarding the grounds of parental obligation. I will make a principled case that parental moral obligations arise exclusively from voluntary acceptance of the parental role. My account explains how parents incur their moral obligations. It is important to note that my findings are not directly applicable to law: there may be policy considerations for holding the mere fact of having procreated, without voluntary acceptance of the parental role, as sufficient for (some) legal parental obligations. But from the moral perspective, understanding parental obligations as connected to socially constructed roles raises problems for the causal account of parental obligations, which holds that causing a child to exist generates parental rights and obligations. More importantly, attention to the institutional nature of the parental role allows us to ask how such a role should be legally and socially constructed, allowing questions of the justice of existing arrangements to arise. From a feminist perspective concerned with the gendered distribution of labour, one major failing of accounts of parental obligations which do not attend to their socially constructed aspect is that they tend to foreclose questions of how such work should be distributed by contributing to the impression that current arrangements are inevitable.

---

generate moral reasons, or because there is a general duty to rescue, the legal parent is now in the best position to rescue the child, no one else will, and so on.

From the moral perspective, one salient question is who holds special obligations to the child. Taking this as starting-point, O'Neill's voluntarist account focuses on how parental obligations are incurred. Parental obligations are special obligations, that is, obligations not owed to every moral patient, but to particular persons. Special obligations are often incurred via voluntary undertakings, as in promising. Thus, O'Neill concludes, 'a standard way of undertaking parental obligations is to decide to procreate', which, in a society where procreators are normally child-rearers, is to decide 'to undertake the far longer and more demanding task of bringing up a child or arranging for its upbringing'.[3] O'Neill leaves unresolved whether involuntary procreators may incur parental obligations as a result of their moral responsibility for the existence of a child. Bayne and Kolers (who term voluntarist views 'intentional') therefore classify her view as a weak intentional account, sufficiency or pluralistic intentionalism, which takes intention as sufficient, but not necessary, for parenthood.[4] My argument will begin, like O'Neill's, by focusing on how parental obligations could be incurred. Unlike O'Neill, I will argue that a voluntary undertaking is necessary, but not sufficient, for moral parenthood.

One further clarificatory point should be made: the voluntarist approach developed here should be distinguished from the intentional account developed by legal theorists in response to legal disputes arising from contract pregnancy. For instance, John Hill argued that the 'preconception intention' of those who 'orchestrated the procreative relationship from the outset' should determine legal parenthood. But Hill's main argument for this actually rests on causality, not voluntarism: except for the commissioning parents, 'who carefully and intentionally orchestrated the procreational act', the child would not have come into existence.[5] Unlike

---

[3] O'Neill, 1979: 26.

[4] See Bayne and Kolers, 2003: 236–8; 2006: 2.3.

[5] Hill, 1991: 359, and see 414–15. For criticism of this argument, see Bayne and Kolers, 2003: 237, and Fuscaldo, 2006: 70. Hill also argues that gestational mothers should keep their promises; but this assumes, controversially, that the transfer of a child can be the subject of promise.

Hill's, my account does not automatically favour commissioning parents. Hill's account has met with much criticism in the bioethics literature. Giuliana Fuscaldo, for instance, rejects it on a number of grounds: it fails to determine parenthood in cases where no one intended to procreate, and it would allow involuntary mothers or fathers to abandon children.[6] While I address some related objections to voluntarism later, I should emphasize that criteria for legal and moral parenthood may differ, and I am not here engaged in identifying legal grounds for parenthood; legal parenthood may be assigned on other grounds than moral obligation.

Defending the Voluntarist Account

My argument begins with the salient fact about moral parents noted above: moral parents have special moral obligations to their children. Special obligations contrast with general obligations; they are owed to particular others as a result of some relationship between the parties. I assume that parental obligations are integral to moral parenthood; one could not occupy the role of moral parent without owing such obligations to the child. Thus, an account of moral parenthood must explain how parental moral obligations are incurred.

I will contend that such obligations must be voluntarily assumed, that voluntarily accepting the social and legal role of parent is necessary for moral parenthood. Accepting the role of parent is conceptually distinct from undertaking to create children. (One could undertake the latter without intending to take on parental obligations, as in contract pregnancy, gamete donation, or carrying out *in vitro* fertilization in a lab.) My case turns on how obligations are incurred. The general outline of my argument is as follows (although the premises will need qualification):

[6] Fuscaldo, 2006: 69–70.

(1) Special obligations only arise through voluntary undertaking or as compensation for some harm.

(2) Parental obligations are special obligations.

(3) Thus, parental obligations are either the result of voluntary undertaking or else owed as compensation for some harm done to the child. (1, 2)

(4) Parental obligations are not compensatory obligations.

(5) Parental obligations arise through voluntary undertaking. (3, 4)

(1) and (4) need defence.

For now, I will only briefly address (1), the controversial voluntarist view that special obligations arise only through voluntary undertakings or as compensation. While this view might seem unappealing, its plausibility—to those who find it plausible—derives from the thought that obligations limit liberty, and liberty can only be limited through choice or as a result of wrong-doing (in act or omission). Voluntarism is criticized on the grounds that there are involuntary special obligations, such as filial duties of loyalty or gratitude or duties of friendship.[7] A distinction between justice and virtue may partly address such objections. Many non-voluntary duties to family members may be duties of virtue, explained through relationship and shared history; unlike parental obligations, they are not correlative to moral rights. It is commonplace to criticize voluntarism in the context of the family as demoralizing: thus one might ask, following Hegel, whether the choice to parent is 'arbitrary', dependent on individual whim. But like John Tomasi, the voluntarist might respond that choosing to parent can only be morally praiseworthy if one has an option.[8] Feminist ethicists have reason to be pulled both ways on this issue. To some, voluntarism seems to ignore a dimension of moral life associated with women's experience, the moral importance of unchosen caring relationships. To other feminists, mindful of how attributions of special obligations

---

[7] See e.g. Austin, 2007: 41–2, and Sommers, 1989.

[8] Tomasi, 1991. See also related discussion in Archard, 1993: 88–93.

within the family sphere have served ideologically to underpin women's oppression, there is reason to be sceptical of an attack on voluntarism premised primarily on intuitions about such obligations. I will return below to the question of whether some family obligations are, indeed, non-voluntary.

Voluntarist approaches, especially in the area of reproduction, are also criticized on the grounds that many agents lack choices, and that voluntarism obscures this by assuming that they do.[9] For example, women's reproductive choices are reduced when they are pressured or forced to have sex, contraception is restricted, abortion is heavily burdened, or they are systematically misinformed about contraception. The decision to become a parent may also be burdened by pressure from a spouse or partner, parents, friends, a pro-natalist society, and so on. Again, the path to parenthood may be an unplanned pregnancy or even the sudden necessity to take on a child due to the death or incapacity of its parents. Below I will offer a more nuanced voluntarist account, which acknowledges these pressures on choice, allowing that parental obligations may issue from tacit voluntary acceptance of the parental role, rather than from a carefully planned and executed intention.

The gist of my argument for (4) is that viewing parental obligations as compensatory reflects an impoverished conception of parenting. Obligations issuing from moral responsibility for causing a child's neediness by bringing it into being are not equivalent to parental obligations. This denial that moral responsibility for a child's existence is sufficient for moral parental obligations is likely to provoke the following objection:

Even if we accept (1), it explicitly allows for the possibility of incurring special obligations involuntarily, when we injure others through recklessness or negligence. Causing certain harms results in special obligations, and a child's neediness is such a harm. Thus, causing a child to exist creates special moral obligations for the morally responsible agents. Those

---

[9] Some of Catharine MacKinnon's comments on rape and abortion could be interpreted thus, if transposed to the moral domain: see MacKinnon, 1989: 171–94.

morally responsible for a child's existence, who are thereby under special moral obligation to it, are moral parents.

The view that causing a child to exist (given that the agent acted freely and that the effect was reasonably foreseeable) entails moral responsibility for the child's existence, and that this moral responsibility generates parental obligations, is the causal account of parenthood.[10]

The causal account itself faces the objection that many people may hold moral responsibility for the existence of a child: biological and commissioning parents, grand-parents, matchmakers, doctors and lab technicians, pro-natalist friends. Causal theorists are aware of this difficulty, which, like Austin, they address with a qualified principle of moral responsibility: 'we possess moral responsibility for the reasonably foreseeable effects of our voluntary actions, when we are the proximate and primary causes of those effects'.[11] The difficulty for the causal theorist then devolves to defining 'primary and proximate cause' so as to rule out lab technicians, and specifying the 'reasonably foreseeable': if birth control promises a less than one per cent chance of pregnancy, for instance, is pregnancy reasonably foreseeable?

A second problem for the causal account is less often noticed: it must explain how moral parental obligations follow from moral responsibility for the existence of a child. I will suggest that there is an explanatory gap between compensatory obligations entailed by moral responsibility for a child's existence, or 'procreative costs', and moral parental obligations, and that this gap is a reason in favour of (4). Moral responsibility for a harm does not, in itself, determine whether compensation is owed or how much is owed. Moral responsibility for a harm does not always entail an obligation to

[10] While the causal account equates causal responsibility (given certain conditions) with moral responsibility for a child's existence, one need not take this view; one might think there is some other way in which agents can be morally responsible for a child's existence. Thanks to David Benatar for this point.

[11] From an unpublished presentation, 'A Causal Account of Parental Obligations', by Michael Austin at the 'Inland Northwest Philosophy Conference', 2006; he defends this view in Austin, 2007: 38–56; compare Fuscaldo, 2006: 71.

compensate, as, for instance, in a case of hurt feelings, where an agent has acted viciously yet violated no rights.[12] Thus, we need to consider both under what circumstances morally responsible agents are obligated to pay compensatory costs, and what those costs should be.

Compensation is not a punitive notion but a rectificatory one. Plausibly, one owes compensation for a harm when one is morally responsible for it (it was intended or reasonably foreseeable) and when the action in question was a rights violation or other serious boundary-crossing harm. This description picks out actions harming the body, (personal) property, or restricting liberty. The harm need not have been intended: negligent and reckless harms may entail compensatory obligations because the negligent agent failed to do something he ought, and the reckless agent undertook an impermissible risk of reasonably foreseeable harm. But if one's rightful conduct harms another by withholding an unowed good, or by failing in civility or kindness, compensation is not owed.

The causal account must make the case that bringing a child into existence is a serious boundary-crossing harm, for which the child is to be compensated. But how is this harm to be construed? One candidate is the child's neediness.[13] Alternatively, one might draw on Joel Feinberg's view that a child has a right to a reasonable assurance of a minimally decent life; if procreators can, but fail to, provide a child such a life, then they have violated this right.[14]

For the sake of argument, let us accept that both neediness and the failure to provide a minimally decent life are harms requiring compensation. There is still an argumentative gap, at least for the

---

[12] Roderick Long suggested in discussion that one can be obligated to compensate without having done something wrong—e.g. taking someone's umbrella accidentally, innocently buying stolen goods. But in these cases we assume the agent has been negligent in some way. If he is truly blameless, it is much less plausible that he owes compensation. Once again, the distinction between law and morality may be helpful here.

[13] See e.g. Austin, 2007: 45. Among the many contributors to discussion on this topic, Silverstein, 1987, and Boonin, 2002: 167–88, argue that procreators should not be held responsible for the child's neediness.

[14] Thanks to David Archard for this suggestion.

neediness point, to the conclusion that parental obligations are compensatory costs. Recall that compensation is a rectificatory notion. The classic doctrine of compensation is that the victim of harm be made whole—that is, restored to her unharmed state or the state she would have been in had the harm not occurred. As an infant's needy state cannot be disentangled from its existence, restoring the child to its prior state or the state it would have been in without the harm is not a permissible option; at best, procreators can remove the child from its harmed state by bringing it to a less needy condition.

Children's neediness consists in the inability to provide themselves with the necessities of life and to avoid harms and dangers. The remedy for the harm of having placed the child in such a position is to enable her to provide herself with necessities, avoid serious harms, and survive independently. Add to this the requirement to provide a minimally decent life. Call this burden of compensation 'procreative costs'. If parental obligations arise as compensation for having placed the child in a needy situation in which its right to a minimally decent life is threatened, then these procreative costs are all that moral responsibility for a child's existence obligates the morally responsible agents to 'pay' by way of compensation.

But these procreative costs are not equivalent to parental obligations, at least as construed, for example, in the contemporary USA. Contemporary parental obligations are extraordinarily weighty in duration and scope. This weightiness is relevant to their incursion. Our society and legal system assign parents a long support period with responsibilities for more than ensuring mere survival to independence and a minimally decent life—more, that is, than procreative costs. Bringing children to self-sufficiency—repairing their neediness—does not include the warmth and affection until late adolescence which parents morally owe to children. Procreative costs could be discharged by providing food, shelter, and basic healthcare, and turning children out of doors as soon as they can survive independently—perhaps as young as 13. What parents owe fluctuates with social change and with the legal institutionalization of parenthood. Compared with past societies, contemporary Western societies and legal systems have increased what parents owe children.[15] Legally, for example, parents are responsible for a much longer period than mere survival requires, they are responsible for ensuring that their children receive education and various vaccinations, and they are prohibited from requiring their children to contribute financially to the domestic economy before a certain age. Socially, not only are parents expected to provide eighteen years of support, warmth, and affection, they are expected to enrich children's lives and seek to enable them to flourish. These expectations are all to the best, but they entail that parental obligations exceed procreative costs.

There is a second gap between procreative costs and parental obligations. In general, compensatory obligations can be contracted out; direct performance is not required. The obligation can be discharged through paying the harmed person, or paying someone else to care for him. This is because compensation relates to the state of the victim, not the compensator. The compensator is simply obligated to restore the victim to the unharmed state. But parental obligation cannot be contracted out; it can only be transferred away. The parent who transfers his child to another through adoption has not contracted out his obligations; he is no longer a moral parent. Parents must personally supervise many aspects of their children's lives. While parents may pay others to share the labour, the parent retains the obligation to coordinate and oversee the labour, and personally supervise the child if needed. Moreover, unlike contractors, parents owe their children a rich, intimate, daily personal relationship; unlike a contractor who oversees (but does not himself carry out) labour, parents must perform a large part of the work of parenting themselves. This relationship cannot be outsourced; there is a serious question as to whether persons who

---

[15] See Alstott, 2004: 49–58.

send their children off at a young age to be cared for by others do inhabit the parental role.

Of course, these extensive obligations reflect contemporary Western conventions. One response open to the causal theorist is to reject these conventions as too extensive, perhaps reflecting an undesirable trend to hyper-parenting. Such an objector might say:

It is supererogatory, not obligatory, for parents to provide more than a minimally decent life. Warmth, personal attention, and promoting the child's flourishing are moral options. Furthermore, parents contract out the care of children, not just for short periods, but to nannies and boarding schools. Such parents might not see their children for years at a time, but they too are parents and fulfil their moral obligations at a distance.[16]

Why should we think parental obligations are not just the procreative costs of ensuring the child is brought to self-sufficiency, and no more?

Certainly, from a feminist perspective, there is room for critique of the parenting norms of our society. But the obligations I have attributed to parents are not gendered nor do they extend to the excesses of parental vigilance: warmth and attention through late adolescence do not constitute hyper-parenting. Still, the causal theorist may wish to argue along the above lines. However, there is a cost to this: the causal theorist taking this line will have to argue for the revision of the parental role in our society. Moreover, given that the requirements of the parental role, as a legal and social institution, vary from society to society, an approach which tries to fix procreative costs to match one specification of this role will presumably leave a gap between procreative costs and parental obligations in a number of societies. Of course, it is open to the causal theorist to take a stand here and critique any societies which exceed (or fall below) his or her account of procreative costs.

---

[16] On the latter point, O'Neill, for instance, describes parents as obligated to make 'some feasible plan for their child to be adequately reared by themselves *or by willing others*'. O'Neill, 1979: 25, my italics; thanks to the editors of this volume for these points.

However, there is a second, more attractive, option for the causal theorist. This is to attack the claim that contemporary parental obligations exceed procreative costs by arguing that those costs just are discharged by taking on socially and legally defined parental obligations, whatever they may be (within the bounds of morality). On this view, compensation just is taking on whatever obligations society assigns parents. In the next two sections, I will make the case that the constructed nature of the parental role raises problems for this approach.

Constructed Parenthood

Parental obligations are institutional, not natural. Law and society define the content of parental moral obligations through the institution of parenthood.[17] The parental role is constructed as a package of specific rights and obligations; through the construction of this role, law and society distribute the burdens of child-rearing between parents and institutions such as educational and healthcare systems. Law and social practice must answer to moral considerations, prohibiting harms and rights violations and meeting children's needs (parents couldn't have a right to treat children as slaves, for example). But practices of rearing children to adulthood can be organized in many ways consistent with morality.

It might be thought that parental obligations are natural, and hence not legally or socially malleable. However, the naturalness of parenthood deserves interrogation, lest, taking a social artefact to be natural, we fall prey to what Mill calls 'that inability to recognise their own work which distinguishes the unanalytic mind'.[18] 'Natural parenthood' is sometimes taken as an independent criterion of

[17] Blustein, 1979, and Zyl, 2002: 112–13, also emphasize the conventional nature of parenthood, as does Archard, 2003: 68–72, with regard to the family.
[18] The phrase appears in Mill's discussion of the social construction of gender; see Mill, 1988: 23.

legal or moral parenthood.[19] But what is natural parenthood? Presumably the term refers to biological parenthood. But if it also suggests family units composed of sexual partners rearing their biological children together, then it conflates social and biological parenthood. The assumption that natural parenthood encompasses care-taking activity imagines that 'natural' parents beget, bear, and rear children in monogamous two-parent, heterosexual families. But this inserts a facsimile of monogamous marriage into 'nature'.

The idea that two-parent families are a feature of human nature, or a prehistoric state of nature, is surely fanciful. For one thing, work in the philosophy of biology suggests that there is no human essence, undermining claims about human nature.[20] Should we turn to the 'natural' world of non-human animals for insight into human nature, we find disconcerting practices of cannibalism, incest, and fratricide.[21] What we know of pre-civil human societies suggests that they featured extended family groupings or polygamy, and hence, group child-rearing. Among historical societies, anthropological variation in family forms undermines the assumption that there is a single 'natural' form. In husband-visitor or extended-family societies, social and biological parenthood are not aligned. In some matrilineal family structures, for example, the child's maternal uncle, not his biological father, takes the male parental role.[22] Even in societies practising monogamous marriage, non-biological social parenting has been common due to high rates of death in childbirth, inability to care for children, and deception regarding paternity.

The claim that parenthood is 'constructed', that its assignment and content depend on convention, might seem strange. Reproduction is, after all, biologically grounded. But the point is that the relation between biological and social parenthood is malleable. Social parenthood is sometimes predicated on biological parenthood, but sometimes also on marriage and other kinship relations.

[19] Bayne and Kolers, 2003: 222–4; 2006: section 2.
[20] See Kitcher, 1999.
[21] See Forbes, 2005.
[22] On these historical and cross-cultural claims, see Shorter, 1976; Coontz, 2006.

Social conventions determine who is eligible to parent a child—the maternal uncle, the biological father, the mother's husband—although the gestational mother has a more constant parental role. Even then, past societies have allowed some gestational mothers to outsource a great deal more parental labour (for example, breastfeeding) than would now be thought consistent with parental obligations.[23]

The last point speaks to the fact that not only does the assignment of parenthood depend on social and legal conventions, but the content of parental obligations depends on how societies divide up child-care responsibilities.[24] Who cares for a child and provides for it, and what such care and provision entail, depends upon convention. Consider matters such as who feeds, clothes, and educates a child, and at what age—and for how long—its care is regularly shared with others. Depending on the society, either the parent or the state may provide healthcare, schooling, school lunches, summer vacations, and day care or baby-sitting. Moreover, our society considers children to become mature and self-supporting at a relatively late age. For example, in Europe prior to the nineteenth century, young men might be thought self-sufficient, and young women marriageable, as young as 13. Today parents are responsible for their children until 18, and they cannot send them out to work or employ them at home instead of schooling them. Expectations of parental involvement and emotional intimacy also differ widely. In the USA in the last fifty years the understanding of a father's role has changed markedly, from a distanced figure to a nurturing, involved one.

Some contemporary parental obligations—such as providing healthcare or nutrition—can be explained as procreative costs. But others—long-term support obligations, warmth, and intimacy—exceed such procreative costs, if those are set at what is needed

---

[23] For an in-depth study of variation in nursing and breastfeeding practices, see Kukla, 2005.

[24] This argument is influenced by Alstott, 2004: 49–58.

to repair a child's neediness and enable it to live a minimally decent life. However, the objection posed above contests this, replying that procreative costs require taking on the social role of parent; procreators who fail to carry out their socially assigned obligations disadvantage their children within that social system. But the constructed nature of the parental role raises a few problems for this objection; at the least, these problems should complicate the statement of the causal account.

First, the mere variability of parental obligations should give pause for thought. At first glance, it seems unfair to parents that the obligations of parenthood should differ so greatly from one society to another. Why should twentieth-century American procreators owe so much more than their eighteenth-century English counterparts? The unfairness is striking because it seems to issue from the costs set by society, and not due to any action on the parents' part. In our socio-economic system, parents are required to do more to prepare a child for self-sufficiency than they have in many other systems. But society—not the parents—is responsible for determining how much a child will need to escape disadvantage. Causing a child to exist causes it to be in need of food, shelter, and so on, to survive; but society causes it to need parental assistance with homework and a high-school education to be eligible for much employment. Parental obligations reflect the way society has coordinated the activities of child-rearing as well as the level of progress of a given society—both of which cause the amount of work assigned to parents to vary. Recall that the causal account assigns obligations to causal parents because they are responsible for a child's state. But my point is that children do not have a fixed amount of needs, but that what they need to flourish depends on society as well as the causal parent. Thus, the causal parent is not solely morally responsible for the child's neediness.

Second, the constructed nature of the assignment of parenthood underscores the difficulty for the causal account of fixing the notion of cause. This account simply does not track parental obligations in matrilineal societies where the maternal uncle is a parent or extended-family societies where a larger kin group parents. Seen in this light, the causal account seems to reflect the heterosexual nuclear-family practices common in contemporary Western society. But from the perspective of different social arrangements, it would not be as obvious as it seems to causal theorists who is responsible for causing the child to exist—its procreators as opposed to the larger clan.

The causal theorist might reply that in matrilineal societies (for instance), the mother's brother who offers his sponsorship to the prospective mother is the relevant morally responsible agent and hence the moral parent. However, the causal theorist taking this line would have to admit that, in our society, a prospective grandparent, or friend, who encouraged procreation and offered to share parental responsibilities would be the moral parent of a resulting child. While this outcome might be acceptable to the causal theorist, it highlights the difficulties of fixing the relevant causal responsibility as narrowly as some causal theorists seem to wish, to (and only to) biological procreators or commissioning parents in artificial reproductive technologies. The causal theorist thus faces a dilemma: either she can narrow the relevant notion of cause to pick out the final steps leading to conception—thus ruling out the mother's brother in a matrilineal society—or she can broaden the notion of cause to include matrilineal uncles, but also pro-natalist friends willing to take part in child-rearing.

A third point is somewhat conjectural. Keeping in mind that the proposed response for the causal theorist is that assuming parental role obligations is required to discharge procreative costs, we should note that role obligations do not typically arise from compensatory obligations. The psychology of role identification explains why this is so. Social role-related moral obligations are not unique to parenthood: doctors, lawyers, nurses, teachers, and spouses take on socially defined obligations with their social roles. While such obligations might be understood as contractually grounded in the choice to take on the role, there is arguably a second way in which social roles ground obligations: taking on a social role involves seeing oneself as an occupant of such a role, and role obligations issue in part from such a self-conception.

Michael Hardimon describes understanding oneself as (among other things) the occupant of a role as 'role identification', in which a role-holder will typically 'conceive of oneself as someone for whom the norms of the role function as reasons'.[25] In role identification, understanding oneself as the occupant of a role shapes one's motivational set: one believes that the fact that one occupies a role gives one reason for doing certain things. This belief may play a role in explaining why one ought to perform the role obligations.[26] As a parent, one may engage in specific activities not because one has specifically agreed to do so, but just because that is what a parent does. While role identification is not a necessary condition for occupying a role (one can become jaded or dissociate from the role), it is a paradigmatic feature of doing so, and its psychology fits better with an origin in voluntary assumption than in the discharge of involuntarily incurred compensatory obligations. This explains why role obligations do not typically arise as compensatory obligations. On the voluntarist account, paradigmatic parents are willing parents; the causal account has no such implication.

That parenthood is a role also explains why its obligations cannot be contracted out with no moral cost, as compensatory obligations can. It matters, morally, that the role-holder perform role obligations herself. The voluntarist can here distinguish between the ideal, in which the parental role-holder fulfils the obligations herself, and a *faute de mieux* arrangement in which (due to temporary incapacity, for example) parental role obligations are carried out by another party. Both might be ways of fulfilling parental role obligations, but the ideal clearly fits the paradigm better than the *faute*

[25] Hardimon, 1994: 358.
[26] A full account, which I cannot pursue here, would have to explain how role identification grounds obligations; I suspect an answer could be given in terms of something like integrity. A condition would have to be, of course, that the role-related obligations are in themselves permissible.

de mieux, or imperfect, arrangement. The causal theorist, it seems, cannot distinguish between these two; the voluntarist can.[27]

The claim that parental obligations are socially constructed does not entail that the relevant social arrangements cannot be criticized—indeed, quite the opposite. From the standpoint of child welfare, we can ask whether given arrangements best protect children's interests. From the standpoint of justice, we can ask whether extant arrangements thwart equal opportunity or gender justice or equality for gays and lesbians. From the standpoint of morality, we can evaluate the permissibility of current laws and practices. The point that the grounds and content of parenthood are culturally relative is not morally relativist; rather, by exposing the conventionality of parenting practices, it opens them to moral analysis and critique. It is instead the appeal to 'natural parenthood' which is unconsciously relativist. The attempt to discern natural relations with an unbiased eye is conducive to the projection of cultural bias, thereby preventing moral evaluation of existing practices.

Voluntary Acceptance and its Limits

If, as I have argued, parental obligations exceed compensatory procreative costs, a voluntary undertaking of those obligations is necessary for moral parenthood. However, voluntarism faces certain problems, as noted above. Does it entail that those who take on the obligations of parenting in unplanned, or constrained, circumstances, are not really parents? When must one decide to become a parent, and must one explicitly decide to take on the parental role and its obligations (or 'decide to procreate', as O'Neill writes)? Could someone act as a parent for several years, then deny she was a parent because, despite her actions, she had never accepted the role?

---

[27] This distinction is drawn from Almond, 2006: 108. Thanks to Avery Kolers for suggesting this point and pressing me to develop the ideas in the previous four paragraphs.

Some role obligations are assumed through explicit agreement—such as wedding vows. But consent to a social role need not be so explicit; it may be given through a process of tacit voluntary acceptance. Tacit voluntary acceptance, as I understand it, should not be equated with tacit consent, if it is thought that the latter may occur without awareness or volition. Although I cannot fully develop an account of voluntary acceptance here, I think, minimally, voluntary acceptance has to involve awareness of the role and its obligations and that what one is doing amounts to entering it, and, further, that one wishes, or intends, or at least believes oneself to be thereby taking on the role. Such tacit acceptance, as contrasted with an explicit statement of intention, is a common route to taking on social roles. Hardimon gives an example of this: he writes that, despite the difficulty of specifying a priori what will count as tacit acceptance of a social role,

it seems plausible to say that once someone has traded her Birkenstocks for Bass Weejuns, her jeans for khakis; once someone has begun to refer to sore throats as 'pharyngitis,' treat patients, and use the medical 'we'; once someone has completed medical school, made her first reservation in the name of doctor so-and-so, and had the letters 'MD' imprinted on her checks—that person has signed on for the role of doctor.[28]

In this example, the doctor takes on her role without a formal acceptance, yet we cannot imagine that, as she gradually takes on the role, she is unaware that she is taking on the role. Nor, though her choice may be constrained (she has to pay back student loans), we cannot imagine that she does not thereby intend to take on the role. Hardimon's account of tacit voluntary acceptance adds nuances to the standard understanding of voluntarism, in which a couple diligently plans to procreate and thereby undertake the parental role; this account allows someone to take on the parental role by thinking something along the lines of 'I guess I'll parent this child, as someone must', and to do so by consciously acting on society's

[28] Hardimon, 1994: 357.

conventions of parenting. Thus, once someone has chosen not to abort, undergone pre-natal medical care, bought some baby clothes, and taken an infant home, the role of parent has been tacitly accepted. In our society, taking a child home as one's own counts as assuming the role of parent—there is no other way to describe this activity, except as baby-snatching. If abortion is an option, then choosing to continue a pregnancy without making plans for adoption constitutes accepting the role of parent.

The publicity of these conventions forestalls the objection that voluntarism would allow someone to take a child home but later deny that she had accepted the role of parent, or all of the parental role obligations. Even if the person has not voluntarily accepted the role, her actions (assuming she knew of the conventions) have triggered parental obligations. The case is similar to that of an infelicitous promise. Acting under the convention of promising results in obligation even if one did not intend to bind oneself; an insincere promise still obligates. Compare the case of a doctor who says later that he did not intend to obligate himself when he said the words of the Hippocratic Oath; his professional moral obligations would still stand. Because knowingly acting under a convention gives rise to obligations despite insincerity, the difficult cases for voluntarism will be those in which someone does not know the conventions; and those cases in which uncertainty is possible, as with some artificial reproductive technologies, therefore call for legal definition.

I have suggested that one comes to occupy a social role through voluntary acceptance. But, as noted above, some critics of voluntarism have suggested that some roles, and their related obligations, are non-voluntary. However, the most plausible case for non-voluntary social role obligations cannot apply to parenthood. Hardimon's account of non-contractual social role obligations appeals to the fact that the relevant roles—family member and citizen—constitute part of our identity because we are born into them. But we are not born into parental roles; we can only take them on later in life.

Voluntary acceptance of parental roles is not sufficient for moral parenthood. There are at least two additional conditions. First, obligations cannot be undertaken if they conflict with already extant parental rights or if the prospective parent is not eligible to parent the child, and second, parents must be reasonably likely to meet a minimum standard of child welfare.

The eligibility criterion reflects the conventionality of the assignment of parental obligations and their content. Social and legal institutions ensure coordination through specifying who is eligible to take on the parental role in the first place. Parental obligations tend to require coordination for their commission, and this coordination is achieved in contemporary Western society through exclusive parental rights. For example, parents need to ensure that a child takes in adequate nutrition and does not fill up on tooth-rotting sweets. To do so, a parent has a right to exclude strangers from feeding the child sweets or even healthy food which may be excessive. This exclusivity reflects conventional assignments of obligations; other arrangements which coordinate the satisfaction of children's needs are possible. In our society, this exclusivity implies that, normally, someone cannot become a parent to a particular child if another person already ably occupies this role. Further, once moral parents have begun to provide care, children's need for continuity of care and (competent) parents' right to pursue their parenting project support such exclusivity. Once moral parents are established, others cannot usually become parents by voluntarily accepting the role.

Second, if ought implies can, an agent cannot take on parental obligations which she cannot fulfil. This does not mean that a parent will cease to be a parent if she is temporarily incapacitated; rather, this is a condition for occupying the role in the first place. Someone might propose a more stringent criterion than merely being able to fulfil parental obligations: the child's best interests. We might imagine a child asking, 'why should sub-optimal parents have power over me, if better parents were willing to assume the obligation?' Once a child has been taken home, this objection loses traction. Children develop attachments to their care-givers; in light of children's developmental needs, a change to 'better' parents could be an overall change for the worse, except in cases of abuse and neglect. However, a child might still ask why, if 'better' parents were available, she was not transferred at birth—before continuity of care began. If birth parents and a rival set of would-be parents both want to take on parental obligations, do the birth parents have a moral claim?

What this objection assumes is a reliable mechanism for identifying 'better' parents. The application of the 'best interests' standard is subject to bias in implementation, such as favouring the wealthy.[29] Not only may attempts at transfer fail to serve children's best interests, but there is an unfairness in transferring children from poorer to richer candidates: parenting is an important project for people who choose it. The interests of those who attempt to become parents, so long as they are competent, should be given weight; deficiencies in ability can be addressed through education and assistance, even licensing, as opposed to redistribution. Transferring infants to those best-placed to rear poses a harm to birth parents which is only justified by severe risk to children. Further, society structures expectations in this regard through specifying eligibility, and these expectations ground legitimate entitlements.

The 'Deadbeat Dads' Objection

A standard objection to the voluntarist account is the involuntary parent. Surely, the objection goes, involuntary fathers owe child support, and involuntary mothers cannot simply abandon their children.[30] Weaker versions of the voluntarist account address this by making voluntary undertaking a sufficient, not necessary, condition for parental obligations, and making moral responsibility for

---

[29] Shanley, 1995: 84.
[30] See Bayne and Kolers, 2003: 238; Fuscaldo, 2006: 69; Austin, 2007: 55.

the existence of the child another sufficient condition.[31] To many, the stronger account seems so absurd as to be its own *reductio*, for it implies that involuntary biological parents do not have moral parental obligations. The intuition that they do is often presented as a conversation–stopper. But relying on this intuition alone risks question-begging. What do involuntary biological parents morally owe?

First, they owe general duties of rescue to the infant. Fuscaldo rejects the voluntarist account because, she says, it allows abandonment of children by involuntary mothers.[32] But if such abandonment endangers the child, the claim that the voluntarist account permits it is false: it would be wrong for anyone to abandon a child to death, because it violates a general duty of rescue. Everyone in a position to save the life of a child has a (prima facie) duty to do so. A biological mother may be uniquely able to save a child, and the voluntarist account does not exempt her from this duty. But parental obligations differ from general duties of rescue. They are not owed by every moral agent to every endangered patient, but by particular adults to particular children.

Second, involuntary procreators may be justly assigned legal duties to their biological children. Legal child support obligations might reflect a compromise between political values. Mandatory legal child support protects single mothers and their children, and this is a strong social justice reason for it. On the other hand, as I have argued elsewhere, social justice reasons pull both ways.[33] For example, some child support collection policies may disproportionately burden the least-well-off men. An account of moral parenthood does not determine who should be legally obligated to support a child; other considerations enter in the legal realm.

Third, there are alternate explanations for strong intuitions that reckless procreators have parental obligations. Austin, for example,

---

[31] O'Neill, 1979, e.g. leaves this possibility open; see also Blustein, 1997.

[32] Fuscaldo, 2006: 69. She refers to legal theory's intentional account, but her objection can be raised to the voluntarist account as well.

[33] See Brake, 2005.

dismisses as 'counterintuitive' the voluntarist implication that (male) repeat procreators or 'deadbeat dads' have no special obligations to their offspring.[34] But 'deadbeat dads' usually describes men who accept obligations and then abandon their families—and such men would have obligations under the voluntarist account. These men differ significantly from an explicitly uncommitted man whose contraception fails. Reckless repeat procreators do indeed arouse moral suspicion. As Oscar Wilde put it, 'To lose one parent may be regarded as a misfortune; to lose both looks like carelessness'. The same goes for the man who repeatedly impregnates women 'accidentally'. But the intuition that he is morally at fault is explicable without assuming that causal fathers have special obligations. Pregnancy has life-altering, sometimes devastating, social, economic, and physical effects on women, and reckless male procreators may be rightly blamed for subjecting them to these. Further, intuitions about 'deadbeat dads' draw on cultural readiness to blame such men. To see this, contrast the 'altruistic stud'—a man who provides sperm to single women who want impregnation. Different intuitions about these cases suggest that morally irrelevant beliefs about sexual behaviour, class, and even race, play a role in such intuitions.[35]

The voluntarist account does not entail that reckless procreators have no obligations. It can hold unintentional procreators to duties of virtue, the duty of easy rescue, legal obligations, and even procreative costs. As procreative costs are explicable within the same moral framework which explains how parental obligations are incurred, the voluntarist account represents a unified and explanatory moral view, not an *ad hoc* set of criteria for parental obligations.

---

[34] Austin, 2007: 46 (in response to the 'no-worse-off' objection) and 55. This intuition plays a large role in Austin's rejection of consent as a necessary condition for parental obligations; ibid. 37 and 45–6.

[35] Such attitudes have been encouraged in the USA following the 1996 PRWORA legislation by campaigns such as the Healthy Marriage Initiative and abstinence-until-marriage education.

'Revolutionary Parenting' and
Justice among Families

Marjorie Shultz argued that legal theory's intentional account, because it separates legal parenthood from opposite-sex couplings, serves feminist goals by accommodating 'alternative' family structures.[36] As Liezl van Zyl pointed out, the intentional account will be biased towards 'traditional' families if it is paired with assumptions that parents are heterosexual and monogamous and that parenthood is inflexibly exclusive.[37] But these assumptions can be altered. Because voluntarism separates parenthood from procreation, it is able to accommodate diverse constructions of parenthood. Moreover, by drawing attention to the institutional nature of parental roles, the voluntarist account allows critique of those roles on the grounds of justice.

One target of such criticism could be the allocation of parental responsibilities. Treating parenthood as a private matter, restricted to the nuclear family, has costs for women and children. When children are treated as an expensive taste, responsibility for them falls primarily on their parents, and disproportionately on women. Proposals for modest collectivism or state support for care-givers address the disadvantages which accrue to care-givers and their children.[38] But there are also non-governmental ways to decrease parental burdens, such as modifying the social conception of the parental role. One way to do so is to spread the burdens among willing individuals. This could involve rethinking the nature of

---

[36] Shultz, 1990; she also argues that the intentional account promotes gender-neutrality by allowing single men to procreate. But as contract pregnancy only allows well-off men to procreate, it gives men the ability to have children while avoiding the burdens of pregnancy and poverty. Nor does the intentional account address the devaluation and exploitation of women's labour. Schultz also claims that the intentional account respects procreative autonomy by allowing reproductive choices to determine legal parenthood. But this is a problematic application of procreative autonomy. Reproductive choice concerns one's own body—not rights over others, such as children.

[37] Zyl, 2002: 116.

[38] See e.g. Archard, 1993; Kittay, 1999; Fineman, 2004; Alstott, 2004.

parenthood—understanding parents not as procreators, but as a network of interested adults and family friends who coordinate care for a child. The voluntarist account may appear counter-intuitive because it diverges from procreation as the criterion of moral parenthood. But this is a benefit; the account takes willing care-givers, not biological parents, as its paradigm.

A concrete example of such an approach is the parenting model which bell hooks has described as 'revolutionary parenting'; taking place among communities of working-class African-American women, revolutionary parenting resembles the extended rather than the nuclear family. Sharing care-taking among a small community helps single and working mothers, and, so long as continuity of care is maintained, such arrangements contribute to child welfare by increasing the number of people acting on the child's behalf and improving the primary care-giver's lot. hooks sees this model as an alternative to the hierarchical dichotomy between legitimate marital and illegitimate unmarried families, and the classism and heterosexism of the nuclear family ideal.[39] Elsewhere, I have argued that liberal principles require state recognition and support of such alternative families if any families are to be so recognized and supported.[40]

The voluntarist account allows for such radical rethinkings of parenting. Multiple unmarried and non-cohabiting adults can become parents simultaneously by accepting the role, and the restriction of parental roles to opposite-sex couples can be criticized on grounds of justice. The flexible and capacious voluntarist account of parenting detaches parenting from procreation and allows criticism of current social conventions of parenting by making them visible.[41]

---

[39] hooks, 1984: 133–46; compare Card, 1996.

[40] Brake, 2010.

[41] Thanks to David Archard, David Benatar, Claudia Card, Marc Ereshefsky, Avery Kolers, Ann Levey, Roderick Long, Bernard Prusak, and Steven Wall for helpful comments on this chapter. Thanks also to participants in the Fall 2008 Joint Colloquium in Bioethics on Role Obligations, and, for research and institutional support, to the Canadian Social Sciences and Humanities Research Council, the Kennedy Institute of Ethics at Georgetown University, and the Murphy Institute at Tulane University.

Bibliography

Allen, Anita, 'Moral Multiculturalism, Childbearing and AIDS', in Ruth R. Faden and Nancy E. Kass (eds.), *HIV, AIDS and Childbearing* (New York: Oxford University Press, 1996).

Almond, Brenda, *The Fragmenting Family* (Oxford: Oxford University Press, 2006).

Alstott, Anne, *No Exit* (Oxford: Oxford University Press, 2004).

Anderson, Elizabeth, 'Is Women's Labor a Commodity?', *Philosophy and Public Affairs*, 19/1 (Winter 1990), 71–92.

Archard, David, *Children: Rights and Childhood* (London: Routledge, 1993).

—— 'John Locke's Children', in Susan M. Turner and Gareth B. Matthews (eds.), *The Philosopher's Child: Perspectives in the Western Tradition* (Rochester, NY: University of Rochester Press, 1998).

—— *Children, Family and the State* (Burlington, Vt.: Ashgate, 2003).

—— 'Wrongful Life', *Philosophy*, 79 (2004), 403–20.

Aristotle, *Nicomachean* Ethics, tr. W. D. Ross, rev. J. O. Urmson (Oxford: Oxford University Press, 1975).

Arras, John, 'AIDS and Reproductive Decisions: Having Children in Fear and Trembling', *Milbank Quarterly*, 68/3 (1990), 353–82.

Austin, Michael W., *Conceptions of Parenthood: Ethics in the Family* (Aldershot: Ashgate, 2007).

Baetens, P., and Brewaeys, A., 'Lesbian Couples Requesting Donor Insemination: An Update of the Knowledge with Regard to Lesbian Mother Families', *Human Reproduction Update*, 7/5 (2001), 512–19.

Barrett, Michèle, and McIntosh, Mary, *The Anti-Social Family*, 2nd edn. (London: Verso, 1991).

Bayne, Tim, 'Gamete Donation and Parental Responsibility', *Journal of Applied Philosophy*, 20/1 (2003), 77–87.

—— and Kolers, Avery, 'Toward a Pluralistic Account of Parenthood', *Bioethics*, 17/3 (2003), 221–42.

—— and —— 'Parenthood and Procreation', in Edward N. Zalta (ed.), *The Stanford Encyclopedia of Philosophy* (Summer 2006 edn.): <http://plato.stanford.edu/archives/sum2006/entries/parenthood/>.

Bell, Nora K., and Loewer, Barry M., 'What is Wrong with "Wrongful Life" Cases?', *Journal of Medicine and Philosophy*, 10 (1985), 127–45.

Bellow, S., *Herzog* (London: Penguin Books, 1965).

Belshaw, Christopher, 'More Lives, Better Lives', *Ethical Theory and Moral Practice*, 6 (2003), 127–41.

Benatar, David, 'Why it is Better Never to Come into Existence', *American Philosophical Quarterly*, 34/3 (1997), 345–55.

—— 'Cloning and Ethics', *QJM* 91 (1998), 165–6.

—— 'The Unbearable Lightness of Bringing into Being', *Journal of Applied Philosophy*, 16/2 (1999), 173–80.

—— 'The Wrong of Wrongful Life', *American Philosophical Quarterly*, 37/2 (2000), 175–83.

—— *Better Never to Have Been: The Harm of Coming into Existence* (Oxford: Clarendon Press, 2006).

Benatar, Michael, and Benatar, David, 'Between Prophylaxis and Child Abuse: The Ethics of Neonatal Circumcision', *American Journal of Bioethics*, 3/2 (Spring 2003), 35–48.

Bigelow, J., Campbell, J., Dodds, S., Pargetter. R., Prior, E., and Young, R., 'Parental Autonomy', *Journal of Applied Philosophy*, 5 (1988), 3–16.

Blackstone, Sir William, *Commentaries on the Laws of England* (1765–9: facsimile of 1st edn., Chicago: Chicago University Press, 1979).

Blustein, Jeffrey, 'Child Rearing and Family Interests', in Onora O'Neill and William Ruddick (eds.), *Having Children: Philosophical and Legal Reflections on Parenthood* (New York: Oxford University Press, 1979), 115–22.

—— *Parents and Children: The Ethics of the Family* (Oxford: Oxford University Press, 1982).

—— 'Procreation and Parental Responsibility', *Journal of Social Philosophy*, 28/2 (Fall 1997), 79–86.

Boonin, David, *A Defense of Abortion* (Cambridge: Cambridge University Press, 2002).

Boswell, John, *The Kindness of Strangers: The Abandonment of Children in Western Europe from Late Antiquity to the Renaissance* (New York: Random House, 1988).

Brake, Elizabeth, 'Fatherhood and Child Support: Do Men have a Right to Choose?', *Journal of Applied Philosophy*, 22/1 (2005), 55–73.

Brake, Elizabeth, 'Minimizing Marriage: What Political Liberalism Implies for Marriage Law', *Ethics*, 120 (2010), 302–37.

Brighouse, Harry, and Swift, Adam, 'Parents' Rights and the Value of the Family', *Ethics*, 117 (2006), 80–108.

Broome, J., *Weighing Goods: Equality, Uncertainty and Time* (Oxford: Blackwell Publishers, 1995).

Buchanan, Allen, Brock, Dan W., Daniels, Norman, and Wikler, Daniel, *From Chance to Choice* (Cambridge: Cambridge University Press, 2000).

Callahan, Daniel, 'Bioethics and Fatherhood', *Utah Law Review* 3 (1992): 735–46.

Card, Claudia, 'Against Marriage and Motherhood', *Hypatia*, 11/3 (1996), 1–23.

Carrier, L. S., 'Abortion and the Right to Life', *Social Theory and Practice*, 3/4 (1975), 398–9.

Cohen, C. B., 'The Morality of Knowingly Conceiving Children with Serious Conditions: An Expanded "Wrongful Life" Standard', in Nicholas Fotion and Jan Heller (eds.), *Contingent Future Persons* (Dordrecht: Kluwer, 1997), 27–40.

Coontz, Stephanie, *Marriage: A History* (London: Penguin, 2006),

Crisp, Q., *The Naked Civil Servant* (London: Flamingo, 1985; 1st publ. 1968).

Dworkin, Ronald, *Law's Empire* (Cambridge, Mass.: Harvard University Press, 1986).

—— *Life's Dominion* (New York: Alfred Knopf, 1993).

Fehige, Christoph, 'A Pareto Principle for Possible People', in C. Fehige and U. Wessels (eds.), *Preferences* (Berlin: Walter de Gruyter, 1998), 508–43.

Feinberg, Joel, 'The Child's Right to an Open Future', in William Aiken and Hugh LaFollette (eds.), *Whose Child? Children's Rights, Parental Authority, and State Power* (Totowa, NJ: Littlefield, Adams, & Co., 1980), 124–53.

—— *Harmless Wrongdoing* (New York: Oxford University Press, 1990).

—— 'Wrongful Life and the Counterfactual Element in Harming', in *Freedom and Fulfilment* (Princeton: Princeton University Press, 1992), 3–36.

Feldman, Fred, *Confrontations with the Reaper* (New York: Oxford University Press, 1992).

Feldman, Susan, 'Multiple Biological Mothers: The Case for Gestation', *Journal of Social Philosophy*, 23 (1992), 98–104.

Fineman, Martha, *The Autonomy Myth: A Theory of Dependency* (New York: New Press, 2004).

Floyd, S. L., and Pomerantz, D., 'Is there a Natural Right to Have Children?', in John Arthur (ed.), *Morality and Moral Controversies* (Englewood Cliffs, NJ: Prentice Hall, 1981), 131–8.

Forbes, Scott, *A Natural History of Families* (Princeton: Princeton University Press, 2005).

Fuscaldo, Giuliana, 'Genetic Ties: Are they Morally Binding?', *Bioethics*, 20/2 (2006), 64–76.

Garcia, Patricia M. *et al.*, 'Maternal Levels of Plasma Human Immunodeficiency Virus Type 1 RNA and the Risk of Perinatal Transmission', *New England Journal of Medicine*, 341 (1999), 394–402.

Glannon, Walter, 'The Ethics of Human Cloning', *Public Affairs Quarterly*, 12/3 (July 1998), 287–305.

—— *Genes and Future People* (Cambridge Mass.: Westview Press, 2001).

Glover, Jonathan, *Choosing Children* (Oxford: Oxford University Press, 2006).

Goodwin, Barbara, *Justice by Lottery*, 2nd rev. edn. (Exeter: Imprint Academic, 2005).

Green, Richard, *Sexual Science and the Law* (Cambridge, Mass.: Harvard University Press, 1992).

Gutmann, Amy, *Democratic Education* (Princeton: Princeton University Press, 1987).

Hall, Barbara, 'The Origin of Parental Rights', *Public Affairs Quarterly*, 13 (1999), 73–82.

Hansen, Michele, Kurinczuk, Jennifer J., Bower, Carol, and Webb, Sandra, 'The Risk of Major Birth Defects After Intracytoplasmic Sperm Injection and In Vitro Fertilization', *New England Journal of Medicine*, 346/10 (7 Mar. 2002), 725–30.

Hardimon, Michael, 'Role Obligations', *Journal of Philosophy*, 91/7 (1994), 333–63.

Harman, Elizabeth, 'Can we Harm and Benefit in Creating?', *Philosophical Perspectives*, 18 (2004), 89–113.

Harris, John, '"Goodbye Dolly?" The Ethics of Human Cloning', *Journal of Medical Ethics*, 23 (1997), 353–60.

Harris, John, 'Rights and Reproductive Choice', in John Harris and Soren Holm, *The Future of Human Reproduction* (Oxford: Clarendon Press, 2000), 5–37.

Hart, H. L. A., and Honoré, Tony, *Causation in the Law*, 2nd edn. (Oxford: Clarendon Press, 1985).

Hershenov, David B., 'An Argument for Limited Human Cloning', *Public Affairs Quarterly*, 14/3 (July 2000), 245–58.

Heyd, David, *Genethics* (Berkeley, Calif.: University of California Press, 1992).

Hill, John L., 'What does it Mean to be a "Parent"? The Claims of Biology as a Basis for Parental Rights', *New York University Law Review*, 66 (1991), 353–420.

Holmes, Helen B., 'Choosing Children's Sex: Challenges to Feminist Ethics', in Joan C. Callahan (eds.), *Reproduction, Ethics and the Law: Feminist Perspectives* (Bloomington, Ind.: Indiana University Press, 1995), 148–77.

Holtug, Nils, 'On the Value of Coming into Existence', *Journal of Ethics*, 5 (2001), 361–84.

hooks, bell, 'Revolutionary Parenting', *Feminist Theory: From Margin to Center* (Boston: South End Press, 1984), 133–46.

Huigens, K., 'Is Strict Liability Rape Defensible?', in R. A. Duff and S. P. Green (eds.), *Defining Crimes: Essays on the Special Part of the Criminal Law* (Oxford: Oxford University Press, 2005), 196–217.

Irvine, William, *The Politics of Parenting* (Saint Paul, Minn.: Paragon House, 2003).

Jeske, Diane, 'Families, Friends, and Special Obligations', *Canadian Journal of Philosophy*, 28 (1998), 527–56.

Jones, Charles, *Global Justice: Defending Cosmopolitanism* (Oxford: Oxford University Press, 1999).

Kahn, Axel, 'Clone Mammals . . . Clone Man?', *Nature*, 386 (13 Mar. 2007), 119.

Kamm, Frances M., *Morality, Mortality* (Oxford: Oxford University Press, 1993).

Kass, Nancy, 'Reproductive Decision Making in the Context of HIV: The Case of Nondirective Counselling', in Ruth Faden, Gail Geller, and Madison Powers (eds.), *AIDS, Women, and the Next Generation* (New York: Oxford University Press, 1991).

Kates, Carol, 'Reproductive Liberty and Overpopulation', *Environmental Values*, 13 (2004), 51–79.

Kitcher, Philip, 'Essence and Perfection', *Ethics*, 110/1 (1999), 59–83.

Kittay, Eva, *Love's Labor: Essays on Women, Equality, and Dependency* (New York: Routledge, 1999).

Kleinman, A., *The Illness Narratives* (New York: Basic Books, 1988).

Kolers, Avery, and Bayne, Tim, '"Are you my Mommy?" On the Genetic Basis of Parenthood', *Journal of Applied Philosophy*, 18/3 (2001), 273–85.

Kukla, Rebecca, *Mass Hysteria: Medicine, Culture, and Mothers' Bodies* (Lanham, Md.: Rowman & Littlefield, 2005).

Lacey, W. K., '*Patria potestas*', in Beryl Rawson (ed.), *The Family in Ancient Rome: New Perspectives* (London: Croom Helm, 1986).

LaFollette, Hugh, 'Licensing Parents', *Philosophy and Public Affairs*, 9/2 (1980), 182–97.

Laing, R. D., and Esterson, Aaron, *Sanity, Madness, and the Family: Families of Schizophrenics* (Harmondsworth: Penguin, 1970)

Larkin, Philip, *Collected Poems* (London: Faber & Faber, 2003).

Levine, Carol, and Neveloff Dubler, Nancy, 'HIV and Childbearing: Uncertain Risks and Bitter Realities. The Reproductive Choices of HIV-Infected Women', *Milbank Quarterly*, 68/3 (1990), 321–51.

Levy, Neil, 'Deafness, Culture, and Choice', *Journal of Medical Ethics*, 28 (2002), 284–5.

Locke, John, *Treatises of Government*, critical edn. with introd. and *apparatus criticus* by Peter Laslett (Cambridge: Cambridge University Press, 1963).

London, Leslie, Orner, Phyllis J., and Myer, Landon, '"Even if you're Positive, you Still have Rights Because you are a Person": Human Rights and Reproductive Choice of HIV-Positive Persons', *Developing World Bioethics*, 8/1 (2008), 11–22.

MacKenzie, Lord, *Studies in Roman Law* (Edinburgh: Wm. Blackwood & Sons, 1862).

MacKinnon, Catharine, *Toward a Feminist Theory of the State* (Cambridge, Mass.: Harvard University Press, 1989).

Macklin, Ruth, 'Is there Anything Wrong with Surrogate Motherhood? An Ethical Analysis', *Journal of Law, Medicine and Health Care*, 16 (1988), 57–64.

McLellan, Faith, 'Controversy over Deliberate Conception of Deaf Children', *The Lancet*, 359 (13 Apr. 2002), 1315.

Macleod, Colin, 'Liberal Equality and the Affective Family', in David Archard and David Macleod (eds.), *The Moral and Political Status of Children* (Oxford: Oxford University Press, 2002).

McMahan, Jeff, *The Ethics of Killing* (Oxford: Oxford University Press, 2002).

Malm, Heidi, 'Paid Surrogacy: Arguments and Responses', *Public Affairs Quarterly*, 3/2 (Apr. 1989), 57–66.

Mill, John Stuart, *The Subjection of Women*, ed. Susan Moller Okin (Indianapolis, Ind.: Hackett Publishing Co., 1988).

—— *Utilitarianism, On Liberty, Considerations on Representative Government* (London: Everyman, 1993).

Mills, Claudia, 'What do Fathers Owe their Children?', in A. Byrne, R. Stalnaker, and R. Wedgwood (eds.), *Fact and Value: Essays on Ethics and Metaphysics for Judith Jarvis Thomson* (Cambridge, Mass.: MIT Press, 2001), 183–98.

Millum, Joseph, 'How do we Acquire Parental Responsibilities?', *Social Theory and Practice*, 34/1 (2008), 78.

Mitchie, S., and Marteau T., 'The Choice to have a Disabled Child', *American Journal of Human Genetics*, 65 (1999), 1204–7.

Mollendorf, Darrell, *Cosmopolitan Justice* (Boulder, Colo.: Westview Press, 2002).

Montague, Philip, 'The Myth of Parental Rights', *Social Theory and Practice*, 26/1 (2000), 47–68.

Mount, Ferdinand, *The Subversive Family: An Alternative History of Love and Marriage* (London: Jonathan Cape, 1982).

Mundy, L., 'A World of their own', *Washington Post* (31 Mar. 2002), W22.

Myer, Landon, and Moroni, Chelsea, 'Supporting the Sexual and Reproductive Rights of HIV-Infected Individuals', *South African Medical Journal*, 95/11 (Nov. 2005), 852–3.

Nagel, Thomas, 'Moral Luck', in Daniel Statman (ed.), *Moral Luck* (Albany, NY: SUNY Press, 1993), 57–71.

—— 'The Problem of Global Justice', *Philosophy and Public Affairs*, 33/2 (2005), 113–47.

Narveson, Jan, *The Libertarian Idea* (Philadelphia: Temple University Press, 1988).

—— *Respecting Persons in Theory and Practice* (Lanham, Md.: Rowman & Littlefield, 2002).

Nelson, James Lindemann, 'Parental Obligations and the Ethics of Surrogacy: A Causal Perspective', *Public Affairs Quarterly*, 5/1 (Jan. 1991), 49–61.

Nicholas, B., *An Introduction to Roman Law* (Oxford: Clarendon Press, 1962).

Nolan, Kathleen, 'Ethical Issues in Caring for Pregnant Women and Newborns at Risk for Human Immunodeficiency Virus Infection', *Seminars in Perinatology*, 13/1 (1989), 63.

Nosarka, S., Hoogendijk, C. F., Siebert, T. I., and Kruger, T. F., 'Assisted Reproduction in the HIV-Serodiscordant Couple', *South African Medical Journal*, 97/1 (Jan. 2007), 24–6.

Nozick, Robert, *Anarchy, State, and Utopia* (Oxford: Blackwell, 1974).

Nussbaum, Martha, 'Reply', in Joshua Cohen and Martha Nussbaum (eds.), *For Love of Country* (Boston: Beacon Press, 1996), 135.

—— *Women and Human Development: The Capabilities Approach* (Cambridge: Cambridge University Press, 2000).

O'Neill, Onora, 'Begetting, Bearing, and Rearing', in Onora O'Neill and William Ruddick (eds.), *Having Children: Philosophical and Legal Reflections on Parenthood* (New York: Oxford University Press, 1979), 25–38.

—— 'Duties and Virtues', in M. Warnock (ed.), *Women Philosophers* (London: Orion Publishing, 1996), 257–72.

Padden, C. A., and Humphries, T. L., *Inside Deaf Culture* (Cambridge, Mass.: Harvard University Press, 2005).

Page, Edgar, 'Parental Rights', *Journal of Applied Philosophy*, 1 (1984), 187–203.

—— 'Donation, Surrogacy, and Adoption', *Journal of Applied Philosophy*, 2 (1985), 161–72.

Parens, Erik, and Asch, Adrienne, 'The Disability Rights Critique of Prenatal Genetic Testing', *Hasting Center Report*, 29/1 (1999), supplement, S1–S22.

—— and —— (eds.), *Prenatal Testing and Disability Rights* (Washington, DC: Georgetown University Press, 2000).

Parfit, Derek, *Reasons and Persons* (Oxford: Clarendon Press, 1984).

Parker, Michael, 'The Welfare of the Child', *Human Fertility*, 8/1 (2005), 13–19.

—— 'The Best Possible Child', *Journal of Medical Ethics*, 33 (2007), 279–83.

Peters, P. G. Jr., 'Protecting the Unconceived: Nonexistence, Avoidability, and Reproductive Technology', *Arizona Law Review*, 31 (1989), 487–548.

Popper, Karl, *The Open Society and its Enemies*, i. *The Spell of Plato* (London: Routledge, 2002; 1st publ. 1945).

Purdy, L., 'Loving Future People', in J. Callahan (ed.), *Reproduction, Ethics, and the Law* (Bloomington and Indianapolis: Indiana University Press, 1995), 300–27.

Railton, Peter, 'Alienation, Consequentialism, and the Demands of Morality', *Philosophy and Public Affairs*, 13/2 (1984), 134–71.

Ratzinger, Joseph, and Bovone, Alberto, 'Instruction on Respect for Human Life and its Origin and on the Dignity of Procreation: Replies to Certain Questions of the Day'. <http://www.vatican.va/roman_curia/congregations/cfaith/documents/rc_con_cfaith_doc_19870222_respect-for-human-life_en.html> (accessed Apr. 2008).

Rawls, John, *The Law of Peoples* (Cambridge, Mass.: Harvard University Press, 1999).

Reeves, R., *John Stuart Mill: Victorian Firebrand* (London: Atlantic Books, 2007).

Robertson, John, *Children of Choice* (Princeton: Princeton University Press, 1994).

Rothman, Barbara Katz, *Recreating Motherhood: Ideology and Technology in a Patriarchal Society* (New York: W. W. Norton, 1989).

Sachs, Jeffrey, *The End of Poverty: Economic Possibilities for our Time* (New York: Penguin Press, 2005).

Sandel, Michael, *The Case Against Perfection: Ethics in the Age of Genetic Engineering* (Cambridge, Mass.: Harvard University Press, 2007).

Savulescu, Julian, 'Procreative Beneficence: Why we Should Select the Best Children', *Bioethics*, 15/5–6 (2001), 413–26.

—— 'Deaf Lesbians, Designer Disability, and the Future of Medicine', *British Medical Journal*, 325 (2002), 771–3.

—— 'New Breeds of Humans: The Moral Obligation to Enhance', *Reproductive Medicine Online*, 10 (2005), supplement 1: 36–9(4).

Scheffler, Samuel, *Boundaries and Allegiances: Problems of Justice and Responsibility in Liberal Thought* (Oxford: Oxford University Press, 2001).

Schieve, Laura A., Meikle, Susan F., Ferre, Cynthia, Patterson, Herbart B., Jeng, Gary, and Wilcox, Lynne S., 'Low and Very Low Birth Weight in Infants Conceived with Use of Assisted Reproductive Technology', *New England Journal of Medicine*, 346/10 (7 Mar. 2002), 731–7.

Sen, A., *Development as Freedom* (Oxford: Oxford University Press, 1999a).

—— 'The Possibility of Social Choice', *American Economic Review*, 89/3 (1999b), 349–78.

Shakespeare, Tom, 'Choices and Rights: Eugenics, Genetics and Disability Equality', *Disability and Society*, 13/5 (1998), 665–81.

Shanley, Mary Lyndon, 'Fathers' Rights, Mothers' Wrongs? Reflections on Unwed Fathers' Rights and Sex Equality', *Hypatia*, 10/1 (1995), 74–103.

Shiffrin, Seanna V., 'Wrongful Life, Procreative Responsibility, and the Significance of Harm', *Legal Theory*, 5 (1999), 117–48.

Shorter, Edward, *The Making of the Modern Family* (Collins: London, 1976).

Shue, Henry, *Basic Rights: Subsistence, Affluence, and U.S. Foreign Policy*, 2nd edn. (Princeton: Princeton University Press, 1996).

Shultz, Marjorie, 'Reproductive Technology and Intent-Based Parenthood: An Opportunity for Gender Neutrality', *Wisconsin Law Review* 297/2 (1990), 297–398.

Sidgwick, Henry, *The Methods of Ethics* (Chicago: University of Chicago Press, 1982; 1st publ. 1874).

Silverstein, Harry, 'On a Woman's "Responsibility" for the Fetus', *Social Theory and Practice*, 13/1 (1987), 103–19.

Smilansky, Saul, 'Preferring Not to have been Born', *Australasian Journal of Philosophy*, 75 (1997), 241–7.

Sommers, Christina Hoff, 'Philosophers Against the Family', in George Graham and Hugh LaFollete (eds.), *Person to Person* (Philadelphia: Temple University Press, 1989), 82–105.

Steinbock, Bonnie, *Life Before Birth* (New York: Oxford University Press, 1992).

Stumpf, Andrea E., 'Redefining Mother: A Legal Matrix for New Reproductive Technologies', *Yale Law Journal*, 96 (1986), 187–208.

Sutcliffe, Alastair G., and Ludwig, Michael, 'Outcome of Assisted Reproduction', *The Lancet*, 370 (28 July 2007), 351–9.

Swift, Adam, *How Not to Be a Hypocrite: School Choice for the Morally Perplexed* (London: Routledge, 2003).

Tan, Kok-Chor, *Justice without Borders: Cosmopolitanism, Nationalism and Patriotism* (Cambridge: Cambridge University Press, 2004).

Thomson, Judith Jarvis, 'A Defence of Abortion', *Philosophy and Public Affairs*, 1 (1971), 47–66.

Tittle, Peg, *Should Parents be Licensed?* (Amherst, NY: Prometheus Books, 2004).

Tomasi, John, 'Individual Rights and Community Virtues', *Ethics*, 101/3 (1991), 521–36.

UNICEF, *The State of the World's Children 2008: Child Survival*, (New York: United Nations Children's Fund, 2008).

Warren, Mary Anne, *Gendercide: The Implications of Sex Selection* (Totowa NJ: Rowman & Allanheld, 1985).

Weinberg, Rivka, 'The Moral Complexity of Sperm Donation', *Bioethics*, 22/3 (Mar. 2008), 166–78.

Westman, Jack, *Licensing Parents* (Cambridge, Mass.: Perseus Publishing, 1994).

Wikler, D, and Wikler, N. J., 'Turkey-Baster Babies: The Demedicalisation of Artificial Insemination', *Milbank Quarterly*, 69/1 (1991), 5–39.

Williams, Bernard, 'Moral Luck', in Daniel Statman (ed.), *Moral Luck* (Albany, NY: SUNY Press, 1993), 35–55.

—— 'Resenting one's own Existence', in *Making Sense of Humanity* (Cambridge: Cambridge University Press, 1995), 224–32.

Working Group on Mother-To-Child Transmission of HIV, 'Rates of Mother-to-Child Transmission of HIV-1 in Africa, America and Europe: Results from 13 Perinatal Studies', *Journal of Acquired Immune Deficiency Syndromes and Human Retrovirology*, 8 (1995), 506–10.

Zyl, Liezl van, 'Intentional Parenthood and the Nuclear Family', *Journal of Medical Humanities*, 23/2 (2002), 107–18.

Index